Better Homes and Gardens.

wiring

Step-by-Step

Meredith® Books
Des Moines, Iowa

TABLE OF CONTENTS

Tools AND MATERIALS 116

Wiring TECHNIQUES 130

Many do-it-yourselfers who wouldn't think twice about building a bunk bed or framing a wall will shrink at the prospect of electrical work. Frantic questions spring to mind: "How do I know the power is really off when I'm working on it? If I make a mistake, will I burn the house down or injure someone?" So they call in a professional electrician for even the simplest repairs, things they could do themselves.

Make no mistake: Electricity deserves respect. But if you are equipped with a basic understanding of how electricity works, and you follow instructions that emphasize safety, you can successfully complete most home electrical projects.

Safety is indeed the most important consideration when approaching a wiring job. In most cases a flip of a circuit breaker and a quick test of the wires for power— a 10-minute job at most—will ensure that you can't receive an electrical shock as you work.

The fact is, a competent homeowner can do many jobs as well as a professional, although probably not as quickly. In fact, for many remodeling installations, the majority of the work lies in opening and covering up walls before and after the actual electrical work—dealing more with carpentry and redecorating than wiring and electricity.

Step-by-Step Wiring explains how your electrical system works and what it takes to tackle most household repairs and improvements. It shows you, in step-by-step fashion, how to fix minor and major problems and how to install new electrical circuits and devices in a professional manner.

Perhaps best of all, *Step-by-Step Wiring* will help you evaluate what you can take on yourself. You'll find that many electrical repairs and improvements are things you can do. If you choose to call in the pros, you'll be equipped to manage the job wisely.

Working to code

Even though you are a do-it-yourselfer working on your own house, you have the same responsibilities as a licensed electrician. You must install electrical systems that will remain safe for many decades. That means using only those techniques and materials acceptable to the building codes of your area.

Local codes vary from place to place, but are based on the National Electrical Code (NEC), published by the National Fire Protection Association, a nonprofit agency. The NEC covers about every conceivable electrical situation. The procedures in this book represent the editors' understanding of the NEC.

Always check with your local building department if you are considering adding or changing your wiring in any substantial way, or if your existing electrical service appears to be substandard. Electrical codes may seem bothersome at times, but they are designed to protect homeowners and keep a home's electrical system running smoothly.

Applying for a permit at your local building department

If you're planning to extend an existing circuit or add a new one, you may need to apply to your building department for a permit and arrange to have the work inspected. Local officials can discuss this with you and explain what jobs require the involvement of a licensed electrician.

If you will be adding new service—not just replacing one fixture with another one—check with your building department before proceeding. Neglecting to do so could cause you the expense and trouble of tearing out and redoing your work.

Your work with the inspector will go better if you follow these guidelines:

Learn as much as you can about each project before you talk with an inspector from your local building department. That way you'll be able to avoid any miscommunication and get your permits more quickly. The department may have information about your type of installation. If not, consult the NEC.

Working with the building department

When you go to the building department, follow these guidelines for a productive visit:

Go to your inspector with a plan to be approved or amended; don't expect the building department to plan the job for you.

Present your plan with neatly drawn diagrams and a complete list of the materials you will be using.

Be sure you clearly understand when you need to have inspections. Do not cover up any work that must be inspected.

Be as courteous as possible. Show the inspector you are serious about doing things the right way, and comply with the requirements.

How to use this book

The first chapter, "Planning for Lighting," discusses one of the major reasons for home electrical work—improving lighting. The next chapter, "Getting to Know Your System," shows how your system works and addresses the other major reason for electrical remodeling—adding electrical capacity and new circuits.

If you plan to do some electrical work yourself, read "Tools and Materials" to get an idea of what equipment you will need for your project. Next read the pages in the "Wiring Techniques" section that apply to the job you have in mind. If you are replacing a light fixture, for instance, you'll want to read "Stripping and Joining Wire" and "Connecting Wires" in that section.

Consult "Troubleshooting and Repairs" to see how to rewire lamps and plugs, repair light fixtures, test and replace switches, and fix almost anything else that can go wrong with your wiring and fixtures. If you want to install new electrical fixtures and service—anything from a new ceiling light to a completely rewired room—you'll find instructions in this book. In "Wiring Improvements" you'll learn how to install a variety of lights and switches, run telephone and cable line, and improve your home's safety with ground fault circuit interrupter (GFCI) receptacles and breakers.

The step-by-step instructions in this book will help you succeed with the most complicated projects—wiring three-way switches, installing switched receptacles and outdoor service, and even planning and adding new circuits.

∧
LIGHT UP YOUR HOME
Installing track lighting can be the first step in enhancing wall displays and brightening your home. The wiring projects in this book will walk you through each step necessary to achieve the result you desire.

Planning
FOR LIGHTING

Improving lighting is a common reason for making changes to a home's electrical system. In older houses, electrical remodeling often focuses on both improving lighting and providing added circuits and electrical capacity. This chapter is filled with ideas to help you improve lighting in your house.

Many of the lights shown draw attention to themselves because they look good. Others, such as recessed lights and modest flush-mounted fixtures, recede visually. Usually a room should have only one or two flashy lights; otherwise it will start to look like a showroom.

Plan lighting with your household activities in mind. Start with *general illumination* (also called ambient lighting) that will give the whole room sufficient light. Then add *task lighting,* directed at a work surface or a table. Make sure the task lights do not glare in people's eyes. Many lights several feet below the ceiling—for instance, a pendent light or a floor lamp—highlight a certain spot while enhancing general lighting. To spotlight an area or a work of art, install *accent lighting* that can be directed precisely.

To make sure you get all the light you want, check a light fixture's bulb wattage rating before you purchase it. Some fixtures take low-wattage bulbs that may not provide the light you're looking for. (And installing bulbs of higher wattage might damage the fixture.)

ACCENT A ROOM

Recessed lighting provides general room lighting while task lights direct light onto the work surface in this home office.

SPOTLIGHTS ACCENT ART

In two little alcoves, halogen spotlights shine on and behind objects of art. The ochre paint of the alcoves turns harsh light warm.

VARIETY OF LIGHTING ENHANCES KITCHEN

This kitchen has many lighting options. A ceiling fixture (not visible) spreads gentle light throughout the room. The pendent light shines on the table and adds to the general illumination. A recessed floodlight in the soffit shines on the open shelves, while smaller fixtures inside the cabinets showcase prized stemware. Undercabinet lighting illuminates the counter and draws attention to the tile work on the wall.

TABLE LAMP LIGHTS PAGES

This table lamp provides little general illumination, but is ideal for reading light.

LIGHTING FOR LIVING AREAS

A bedroom or living room typically has a single flush light fixture in the center of the ceiling; in a dining room this light may be a chandelier or other type of pendent light. Although this is fine, you will be happier with a more creative arrangement that enhances the way you live.

Adding more illumination can have positive results. Many families have become used to living in a dimly-lit room. Once brighter light is added, they are surprised by the room's pleasant atmosphere.

Living rooms and family rooms (or great rooms) almost always benefit from layers of lighting. It's a good idea to supply two types of general (ambient) lighting. This can include a single flush light or chandelier in the center of the room, plus track lighting or a grid of recessed lights running around the room's perimeter.

Add one or two fun lights, even if you use them only occasionally. Accent lighting in a cabinet can showcase glassware or china. A spotlight placed on the ceiling near the wall can point down and graze the wall, perhaps to accent a textured surface. Euro-style lights suspended from wires or snaking around a ceiling in a curved track add a touch of whimsy.

Dimmer switches are often a good idea, even if you usually only turn a light on and off. Some dimmer switches can turn a light on and off at a prescribed level of illumination, so you don't have to fiddle with the brightness each time.

Table and floor lamps are an important part of the lighting plan. If you wire the receptacle so it is controlled by a switch (see page 95), you can control the lamps with a regular or dimmer wall switch.

If a dining room table is nicely lit, people will be more likely to linger and talk. A pendent light is the usual choice. Make sure the table is well lit but that the light does not shine in people's eyes.

An entry area should be lit brightly but warmly; consider a light fixture with a globe that is slightly yellow rather than white. Usually a single fixture is enough.

LAMPLIGHT
An ample supply of table and wall lamps can light up a room without overhead lighting. In this situation it's a good idea to have at least some of the lights plugged into receptacles that are controlled by a wall switch.

<

LIGHTING TO DEFINE AREAS

In an open layout, where one room flows into another, intimate lighting fixtures can establish a room as its own separate place.

ʌ   >

LIGHTS ADD COZINESS

Twin pendent lights on either side of a bed make for pleasant nighttime reading. The yellow colors on the walls and fabrics, as well as the wood accents, make the lighting feel warm and embracing.

SCONCES SAVE THE VIEW

Here the ceiling is too high for a flush ceiling fixture, and a chandelier would block the view of some stunning windows. The solution: wall sconces, located at two heights, carry much of the lighting load. Where the ceiling is lower, swiveling recessed fixtures take over.

LIGHTING FOR KITCHENS

A well-lit kitchen makes food preparation more enjoyable and welcomes family members and guests. Many kitchens include an eating area, which should be lit separately, as you would a dining room table.

Overhead lighting should provide both general and more specific lighting. Consider installing one flush light in the center of the room (two if the room is long rather than square), and run a series of recessed or track lights around the perimeter, about 2 feet away from either the wall or the wall cabinets. For a dramatic touch that also adds good general illumination, install cove lighting—inexpensive fluorescent fixtures that sit on top of wall cabinets.

Undercabinet lighting is essential.

The underside of a wall cabinet is typically 54 inches high, just the right height for lighting a countertop without glare in the eyes of an adult standing at the counter. To make the lighting comfortable for children, install lenses that cut the glare.

Make sure the kitchen sink is well lit. If it is in front of a window, position a recessed or track light directly above and near the wall so the person doing dishes will not cast a shadow.

To grow herbs or other plants in a kitchen window, natural light may not be enough, especially during the winter. Add a fixture that uses incandescent bulbs or fluorescent tubes made for helping plants grow. They may be labeled "full-spectrum" or "grow-light."

> **LIGHT FOCUSES ON WORK AREAS**
> Downlighting from recessed fixtures lights kitchen work surfaces without distracting glare.

> **WINDOW IS PART OF PLAN**
> Don't forget to include the sun in your lighting plans. Most people like having the sink in front of a window. Here, an extra-large window fills the kitchen with light.

FIXTURES ADD STYLE
Black track lighting and an eye-catching chrome pendent light add to this sleek Euro style.

LIGHTS LOOK RIGHT
Standard recessed fixtures would look out of place in this cozy kitchen; by adding an unusual hanging glass trim, they feel right at home. The undercabinet fluorescents use full-spectrum tubes for warm illumination.

LIGHTING FOR BATHROOMS

A bathroom must be brightly lit and the light should not be harsh. A modest-size bathroom should have an overhead fan/light fixture, plus lighting for the mirror above the sink. A large bathroom benefits from one or more additional ceiling lights, perhaps directed at a second mirror.

Lights on either side of the mirror clearly illuminate a person's face. Lights above the mirror often cast shadows, especially on a person's neck. Choose nonglaring lights; several low-wattage decorative bulbs usually work well. Fluorescent lights are a good choice, as long as they have glare-reducing lenses and you install warm-toned tubes. Some medicine cabinets have built-in lights, which you may be able to test for lighting effects at the store.

Spend a bit more for an overhead fixture that has all the features you need. Buy a vent fan powerful enough to suck moisture and odor out of the room (see pages 100–101). Some models have night-lights that come on when it gets dark so you can find your way without stumbling. A unit with a heat lamp or a heating unit with a fan provides extra warmth while you are drying off.

Make sure the tub/shower will be well lit, both during the day and at night. If you have a glass shower door or use a sheer shower curtain, the overhead fixture may provide enough light. However a watertight recessed light over the tub/shower is usually a good idea, especially if the room does not have a window.

LIGHTS MATCH CABINETS
Inexpensive bathroom wall fixtures are available in styles to match most cabinetry and sink arrangements. Here floral-shaped globes, with decoratively curved metal tubes and a natural wood base plate, suit the bathroom's old-fashioned feel.

MIRRORS BRIGHTEN BATHROOM LIGHTING
Large mirrors in a bathroom can nearly double the effect of the lighting. The fixtures in the shower area must have waterproof lenses.

BRIGHT AND STYLISH BATH

Lighting can help turn a bathroom into a style statement. Here the ceiling has high-gloss paint to reflect the light from a pendent fixture. The mirror has shaded sconces on either side and overhead recessed spotlights. Wall cabinet lighting filters down through glass shelves.

OUTDOOR LIGHTING

Exterior lights can serve four functions: They discourage intruders, improving security; they help you get around without tripping; they beautify your yard at night; and they create the right mood for evening dining and other activities. To accomplish these goals, a variety of lights should be placed on a house's exterior, along paths, in the yard, and on a deck or patio.

Standard-voltage fixtures provide bright light, so you should have at least one on the house's exterior, and perhaps one in the yard or above the garage door. Running new cable for these lights is a difficult task; low-voltage lights are much easier to install (see pages 96–97). The light they provide is not bright, but it is often sufficient for most purposes.

There are plenty of switching options to choose among. A timer turns lights on and off at specified times. A photocell turns lights on at night and off in the day. A motion-sensor switch turns the light on for a prescribed amount of time when someone walks in its path. All these can be overridden by a manual switch when you choose.

A potential burglar will likely be frightened away by bright light, especially if surprised by a light that comes on via a motion-sensor switch. See that all points of access— windows as well as doors—are well lit. Floodlights are most effective and should be placed where it is difficult for an intruder to reach them to remove the bulb.

> **LIGHTS ADD BEAUTY AND INCREASE SAFETY**
A gazebo lit with bright standard-voltage overhead lights as well as strings of decorative lights around the two roofs looks inviting. Low-voltage riser lights make it easy to climb the steps without tripping.

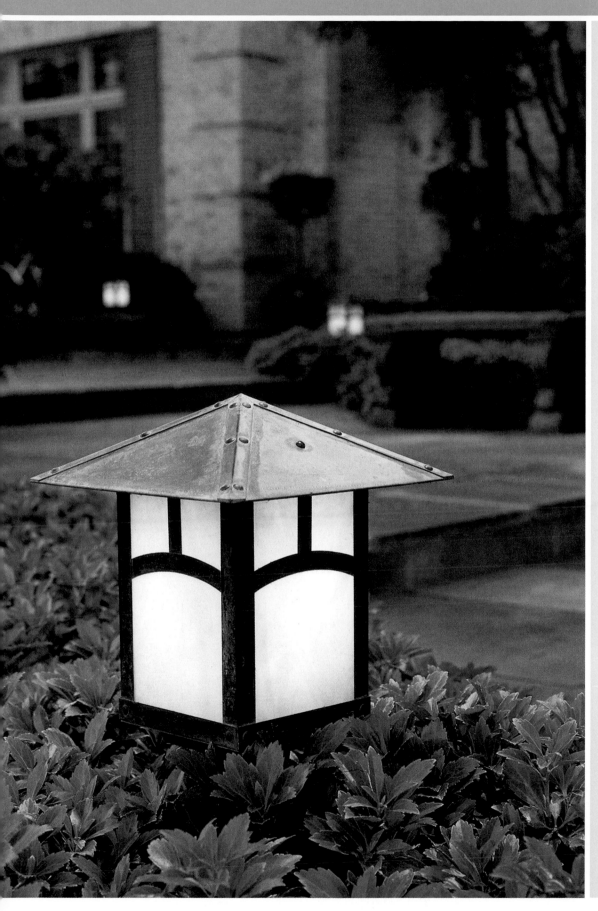

<

**LOW-VOLTAGE
LIGHTS HAVE
HIGH STYLE**
Many newer low-
voltage lights have
stylish metal covers
and frosted glass
lenses. They are
just as easy to
install as the older
plastic types.

Getting to Know
YOUR SYSTEM

Your house's wiring may look complicated (and frightening), but it's not as difficult to comprehend as you may think. This chapter will help you understand your system so you can make informed decisions about remodeling or adding new service and can be sure the system is safe. It also shows the appropriate steps to take to correct unsafe conditions.

Before you embark on a wiring project, read through the chapter to gain a general understanding of electrical principles and basic household wiring configurations. The following pages will show you how to avoid the danger of electrocution, as well as how to open up electrical boxes with confidence. You'll also learn how to conduct an inspection of your system to make sure it is safe.

This book deals with the most common types of electrical installations. Be aware, however, that not all household systems are installed safely. Especially if you have an older home, it is possible that some work has been done incorrectly or does not meet current codes. The result could be dangerous.

When working on your system, you should always understand what you are opening or dismantling. If at any time you suspect you are delving into the unknown, at least be sure the power is turned off. If you see wiring or boxes that have not been described in this chapter, call in a professional electrician for an evaluation.

CIRCUITS THAT MAKE SENSE

In a well-organized electrical system, all the lights in a room—even when there are many different types, as in this kitchen—are controlled by the same circuit. Receptacles are typically on one or two separate circuits.

BATHROOM HAS SAFE OUTLET

Most electrical codes require a bathroom's receptacles to be on a separate circuit, since blow-dryers and other high-wattage appliances often plug into them. Receptacles near a sink should be GFCIs for shock protection.

SEVERAL ROOMS MAKE A CIRCUIT

Because they do not use much amperage, lights from living rooms, dining rooms, and bedrooms are often on a single circuit. Low-voltage halogen lighting, though bright, uses little electricity.

The primary rule of electrical work is simple but vital: Before dismantling or touching wiring, always shut off the power, then test to make sure the power is off.

This page shows the most common ways to shut off power and test for power using a voltage tester. See pages 20–21 for other types of testers. You may want to use a voltage detector to double-check, or to test for power before you open a box.

Take steps to remove all distractions while you work on wiring. Keep children away from the area where you are working. Also turn off the radio and the TV so you can focus on the task at hand.

To be doubly safe, act as though the power is on even when you know it is off. Wear gym shoes or other shoes with rubber soles. Use tools made specifically for electrical work. These typically have generous rubber grips, so you never need to touch metal. Remove any jewelry or a watch. If you are working in the basement, stand on a wooden platform rather than concrete, especially if it is wet. Use a non-conducting ladder (fiberglass is a good choice) rather than a metal ladder.

CAUTION

THE DANGERS OF HOUSEHOLD CURRENT

If you are standing in a dry place wearing rubber-soled shoes, a shock from a standard 120-volt circuit will certainly get your attention, but it will probably not seriously hurt you. However, if you have a heart condition, or if you are standing on a wet surface or a metal ladder, 120 volts can injure you. And 240-volt current will likely do serious harm no matter what you are wearing. Keep in mind children are in grave danger from any sort of shock.

SHUT OFF POWER TO A SINGLE CIRCUIT.

In most cases it is sufficient to shut off power only to the circuit being worked on. To do this, flip a breaker or remove a fuse. (See pages 24–25 for more information about the service panel.) If your service panel is well indexed, you can easily find the circuit. Be aware, however, that the label may be incorrect, so always test for power after turning it off.

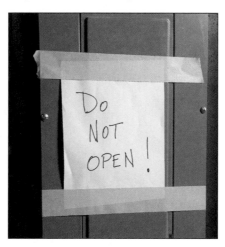

SEE THAT THE POWER STAYS OFF.

To ensure that nobody restores power while you work, tape a note to the box. For greater security, lock the panel; most service panels have a place for a padlock.

SHUT OFF POWER TO ALL CIRCUITS.

For major projects, or if you are unsure which breaker or fuse controls the wiring you will work on, shut off power to the entire house. In most cases the main breaker or fuse is located at the top of the panel. Be aware that even after you have shut off the main breaker, the wires entering the box from outside the house are still live.

TEST FOR POWER.

Test a receptacle for power by inserting a voltage tester's probes into the slots. You can also use a receptacle analyzer or a multitester. To test a switch's wiring, a ceiling fixture, or a junction box for power, remove the cover as shown on the opposite page and touch the probes to the bare ends of a white wire and a colored wire.

In a safe, code-approved electrical system, all wires (as opposed to cable, which encloses two or more wires) are securely encased in an electrical box. Most electrical projects require that you open a box to get at the wiring. As long as you take the proper precautions, you can do this safely.

Shut off the electricity to the circuit and do a preliminary test for power: use a tester to check a receptacle for power, or flip a switch to see if a light comes on. Be aware, however, that power may still be present in the box even if this initial test is negative. So proceed cautiously, following the safety tips on the opposite page.

1 REMOVE THE COVERPLATE.

After testing to see that the power is off, remove the coverplate's screws—one for a receptacle cover and two for a switch cover—using a small slot screwdriver. If the coverplate does not come off easily, gently pry with the screwdriver, taking care not to poke the blade in more than ⅛ inch.

2 PULL OUT THE DEVICE.

Unscrew the mounting screws until the device is free (the screws will probably not come all the way out). Hold the device by the plastic part only, and gently pull outward. Test all exposed wires for power; it is possible that power from another circuit is traveling through the box.

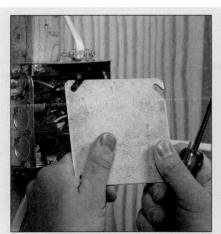

OPEN A JUNCTION BOX.

Junction boxes often contain power from more than one circuit, so use a voltage detector to check all the cables as well as the box itself (see page 20). The coverplate may be metal or plastic. Typically you need to remove one screw and loosen the other to remove the coverplate. Once it is open, double-check for power using a voltage tester.

OPEN A CEILING FIXTURE.

After flipping the switch to see that the power is off (make sure it's not just a burned-out bulb), loosen the setscrews and remove the glass or plastic globe. Remove the bulbs. Usually the canopy is held in place by either two mounting screws or a center nut. Remove the screws or nut, and gently pull the fixture down. If it is heavy, support it with a coat hanger (see page 62).

OPEN A SERVICE PANEL.

Open the panel's door, and flip off the main breaker or remove the main fuse. To get at the panel's wires, remove the mounting screws, which may be on the face of the cover or on the sides of the box. Remove the cover.

USING TESTERS

Keep a reliable voltage tester close at hand at all times, and make it a habit to test for power at the beginning of every project.

Become comfortable using your tester so you can make firm contact with both probes while looking at the tester's indicator. In many cases you'll have to hold both the tester and one probe, or both probes with one hand. Alternatively you can allow the tester to dangle while you hold one probe in each hand.

Be sure both probes make firm contact with bare wire or other metal—not the plastic insulation. If the metal is painted, test, then scrape the paint away, then test again. When testing a receptacle, insert the probes all the way in.

RECEPTACLE ANALYZER.

Just plug it in. A receptacle analyzer will tell you if the power is on and whether the receptacle is properly grounded and polarized (see page 26).

VOLTAGE TESTER.

For standard 120-volt power, touch the probes of a voltage tester to one black (or colored) wire and the white wire (or the terminals the wires are connected to); or to the black wire and the electrical box, if it is metal.

VOLTAGE DETECTOR.

Hold a voltage detector near or up against an electrical box, a fixture, or a cable. When you press the button, the detector will glow if power is present. A voltage detector can often sense power inside a wall, but not always.

ELECTRONIC SCANNER.

A multifunction scanner senses the presence of studs, pipes, and electrical cables inside a wall. It can also act like a voltage detector, telling you if power is present in cables. If you have plaster walls (rather than drywall), it may not give reliable readings.

TESTING A 240-VOLT RECEPTACLE.

Use a four-level tester or a multitester to check a 240-volt receptacle. When you insert the probes into the receptacle's two vertical slots, the tester should register 240 volts. Inserting into one vertical slot and one other slot should yield a reading of 120 volts.

TESTING A SWITCH FOR CONTINUITY.

Disconnect power before using a continuity tester. To test a two-way switch or a special switch (see pages 122–123), grab one terminal or wire end with the clip, and touch the probe to the other terminal or wire end. The tester should glow when the switch is turned on, and not glow when the switch is off; otherwise replace the switch.

TESTING A THREE-WAY SWITCH.

To test a three-way switch, fasten the tester's clip to the dark common screw terminal, and touch the probe to one of the other terminals. If the tester glows when you flip the switch to one position and stops glowing when you flip it to the other position, the switch works properly.

TESTING A CARTRIDGE FUSE.

Hold a continuity tester's clip against one end of a cartridge fuse, and touch the probe to the other end. If the tester glows, the fuse is good. If not, replace it.

TESTING LAMP WIRING.

Dismantle a lamp and pull out the wires so you can tell where they travel. Using a continuity tester, clip one end of a wire, and touch the other end with the probe. If the tester does not glow, the wire is broken somewhere and should be replaced.

MULTITESTERS.

A multitester performs several functions and can take the place of several testing devices. Use it to test 120-volt circuits, 240-volt circuits, and low-voltage wiring. It is an essential tool for some appliance repairs (not covered in this book) because it tells you precisely how much power is present. It also tests for continuity and resistance. A digital multitester is easier to use than an analog multitester.

HOW CIRCUITS WORK

E lectricity is the flow of electrons through a conductor. In home electrical systems, wires, consisting of highly conductive copper wrapped in insulation for safety, are the conductors that carry electricity. A host of other items, such as a fork, screwdriver, or even yourself, can also serve as conductors, sometimes with disastrous results. A safe electrical system will prevent this from happening.

Electricity always flows in a loop, known as a circuit. When a circuit is interrupted at any point, the electricity shuts off. As soon as the circuit is reconnected, the flow begins again.

Your local electric company distributes electricity generated at power plants. Overhead and underground wires bring power from the utility company lines to a home's service head, also called a weather head because it keeps rain and snow from entering. Although the utility company sends high-voltage electricity along some of its power lines, by the time it reaches your house, it has been reduced to 120 volts per wire.

The electricity passes through an electric meter, which measures how much enters the house. It enters a service panel (also called the breaker box or fuse box), which distributes electricity throughout the house along individual circuits. Each circuit flows out of the service panel, through a number of fixtures and receptacles, and back to the service panel. (For more on service panels, see pages 24–25.)

In a circuit, electricity flows out of the service panel on *hot* wires that usually have black insulation, although sometimes they may be red or other colors. Electricity returns to the panel on *neutral* wires that have white insulation.

The service panel contains circuit breakers or fuses. These safety devices

FOLLOWING THE FLOW.

The flow of electricity in typical household circuits starts with the two 120-volt lines and single neutral line that enter the top of the service panel. Both 120-volt lines make the 240-volt circuit, though only one

neutral line is needed for the circuit. The 120-volt circuit has one hot wire (black) and one neutral wire (white), plus a copper ground wire (green). In case of a short, the ground wire carries the current safely into the earth.

shut off the power in case of a short circuit or other fault in the circuit (see pages 24–25, 51–52).

Each circuit has branches, which might be receptacles, fixtures, or switches. A wall switch, for example, interrupts (off) or completes (on) a branch to one or more light fixtures. Some appliances, such as a dishwasher, disposal, or microwave oven, may need their own circuit.

Most circuits carry 120 volts. This will give you quite a jolt if you accidentally come into contact with it, but it should not cause serious harm. Most homes also have one or two 240-volt lines, which use two hot wires and one neutral wire to double the power. Because of the higher

power, be cautious when dealing with these lines.

Every electrical system should be grounded for safety. Usually this is done by connecting a wire from the service panel to a cold-water pipe or a grounding rod sunk deep into the earth. Sometimes both grounds are used. Grounding diverts current harmlessly into the earth in case of a circuit fault.

Circuits in your home may have a grounding wire that is bare copper or green. Some fixtures and devices are grounded through the metal receptacle boxes and the metal conduit that contains the wires (see page 26).

Light fixture

Wall switch

Service head or weather head

Service wires (If you have only two rather than three, see page 32.)

Receptacles

Electric meter

Service panel

Grounding rod

Air-conditioning unit requires 240 volts.

Electrical projects always begin at the service panel, which is either a breaker box or a fuse box. When a short or an overload shuts down power to a circuit, this is where you go to restore the flow. It's also where you cut off power to a circuit before starting a project.

Power arrives from the meter through two main power wires, each carrying 120 volts into the house. Usually these are black and/or red. A white main neutral wire completes the circuit. These incoming hot wires connect to a main power shutoff. When you turn this off, the incoming wires above the main shutoff remain hot, but there is no power to the fuses or breakers for branch circuits.

Breaker boxes

A breaker box's main shutoff connects to two hot bus bars. Each 120-volt breaker attaches to one of the bars. (This means that if one of the main hot wires gets damaged outside your house, you will lose power to about half of the circuits in your house.) Each 240-volt breaker attaches to both bus bars. When a circuit is overloaded or a short occurs, an element in the breaker heats up and causes the breaker to trip and shut off power before the wires heat up and become a danger.

The main neutral wire connects to the neutral bus bar. This bar is connected to a system ground wire, which leads to a grounding rod. White wires for every circuit, and sometimes bare or green ground wires, connect to the neutral bus bar. As a result each 120-volt circuit has a black or colored wire leading from a circuit breaker and a white wire leading to the neutral bus bar. A bare copper or green-covered ground wire may also connect to the neutral bus bar. Each 240-volt circuit has two hot wires connected to the

circuit breaker. The 240-volt circuit also has one neutral and, possibly, a ground wire, connected to the neutral bus bar. Systems with conduit or armored cable do not necessarily need separate ground wires—the conduit or metal sheathing can act as the ground conductor.

Instructions for troubleshooting circuit breakers and checking for the cause of shorts are on page 51.

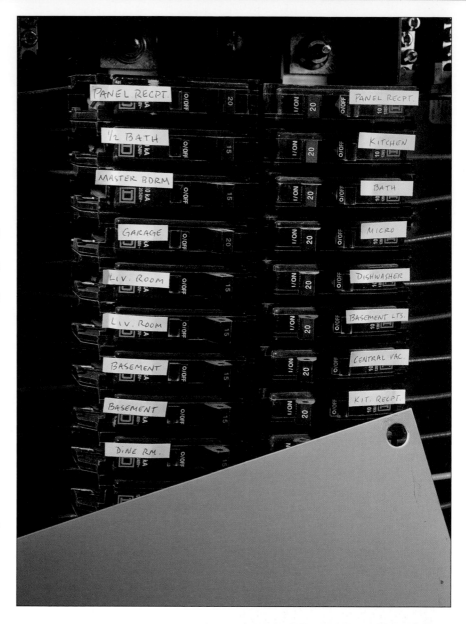

CAUTION

LEAVE INCOMING WIRES FOR THE UTILITY COMPANY

If you suspect that the wires entering your house may be damaged in any way, do not attempt to work on them your-self. Have the utility company inspect them. Usually they will inspect and repair them for free.

Fuse boxes

If you have an older home that has not been rewired in the last 25 or 30 years, chances are that its electrical heart is a fuse box rather than a breaker box.

Fuse boxes are wired and work the same way as breaker boxes (opposite page), but instead of tripping as a breaker does, a fuse "blows" when there's too much current in its circuit. When this happens, you must eliminate the short or the overload, remove the blown fuse, and screw in or plug in a new one.

As with a breaker box, electricity enters through two main power wires. (In a house with no 240-volt equipment, there may be only one power line.) The current flows through a main disconnect, in this case a pullout block that holds a pair of cartridge fuses.

A series of plug fuses protects the hot wires of the individual circuits, often called branch circuits. Unscrewing a fuse disconnects its circuit. A neutral bus bar receives the main neutral wire as well as all the neutral wires for the branch circuits. A system ground wire leads from the neutral bus bar to a grounding rod outside the house.

For tips on troubleshooting a fuse box, see page 52.

Main neutral wire
Main power wires
Neutral bus bar
Plug fuses
System ground wire
Cartridge fuse
Pullout block

TYPICAL PLUG FUSE.

A plug fuse is threaded and screws into the fuse box. Handle only the rim. Do not touch the threads while removing or replacing the fuse. For information on identifying and replacing a blown fuse, see page 52.

HANDLING PULLOUT BLOCKS.

Larger 240-volt circuits, as well as main shutoff fuses, often are protected by pullout blocks that contain cartridge fuses. If you need to pull out a cartridge fuse that is not in a pullout block, do not use your fingers—you could touch the live end. Get a fuse puller (see page 52).

⚠ CAUTION

NEVER UPGRADE A FUSE

If you have a chronically overloaded circuit, you might be tempted to install a bigger fuse, such as replacing a 15-amp fuse with a 20-amp fuse. Don't do it. Wiring that gets more current than it was designed to handle heats up and can catch fire. Always replace a blown fuse with one that has the same amperage rating.

Older homes often have ungrounded receptacles and fixtures, and many local codes do not require rewiring them so they're grounded. Grounding is still worth adding to your system, though, because it adds protection against electrical shock. Grounding provides a third path for electricity to travel along, so if there is a leak, current will flow into the earth rather than into the body of a person who touches a defective fixture, appliance, or tool.

An electrical system is grounded with a grounding rod driven at least 8 feet into the earth outside the house or connected to a cold-water pipe. Each individual branch circuit must be grounded as well, either with a separate wire that leads to the neutral bus bar of the service panel or through metal conduit or cable sheathing that runs without a break from each box to the panel.

In some locations in your house—especially where the outlet or appliances may become wet—GFCI (ground fault circuit interrupter) receptacles are required (see pages 76–77). Older, ungrounded circuits are usually polarized, which is less effective than grounding but better than nothing. Grounded and polarized receptacles provide protection only when wired correctly. Use a GFCI receptacle analyzer to test for this (page 49).

CAUTION

DON'T ALTER PRONGS ON PLUGS

Never clip or file down the prongs on a grounded or polarized plug. Go to the heart of the problem: Test and upgrade your circuit and receptacle.

A POLARIZED RECEPTACLE.

A polarized outlet has one slot that is longer than the other. This ensures that when a polarized plug is inserted, the hot and neutral wires in the cord connect to the correct wires in the circuit. Although not as safe as a grounded system, polarization does add a measure of safety.

The grounded box safely carries away the electricity from the loose wire.

A GROUNDED RECEPTACLE.

The grounding circuit must follow an unbroken path to the earth. A third, rounded prong on modern plugs fits into the ground slot in the receptacle. This slot connects to a wire—or to the metal box and conduit or sheathing—that leads uninterrupted to the neutral bus bar of the breaker box. The system ground wire then connects the bus bar to the earth. Often a cold-water pipe is used for grounding instead of a grounding rod because it connects to water supply pipes deep under the ground.

SWITCH AND RECEPTACLE WIRING

This page and the next will help you understand the wiring you will see when you open a switch or receptacle box. The wiring is not always straightforward at first look. You will often find several wires going to a receptacle, and perhaps exiting the box to travel to the next receptacle. This page and the next will show some usual wiring for switches and receptacles.

GROUNDING METHODS

The wiring arrangements shown on this page and the following one emphasize the hot and neutral wires. Also pay attention to how the devices are grounded. Receptacles should always be grounded. Grounding is recommended for switches and lights, but many systems omit this. If the device's box is plastic, a ground wire should connect to the device. If the box is metal, the most secure arrangement is to attach ground wires to both the device and the box. In some systems a ground wire attaches only to the device. If the circuit has metallic armored cable or metal conduit, the metal box can act as the ground, eliminating the need for a ground wire.

If your appliance or tool has a plug with a third, round prong, it should only be plugged into a properly grounded three-hole outlet (see opposite page). Some appliances and tools are double insulated and do not need the extra protection of a grounding prong. You can plug them into an ungrounded outlet and still be protected from an electrical shock.

THROUGH-WIRED SWITCH.

If power comes into the switch box first and then goes to the fixture, the neutral (white) wire travels directly to the fixture, and the hot (black or colored) wire flows through the switch. When flipped on the switch allows power to flow; when flipped off it interrupts the flow of power.

END-WIRED SWITCH.

If power flows directly to the fixture, a two-wire cable leads from the fixture to the switch. One wire connects to the hot wire in the fixture box and the other wire connects to the fixture's hot wire so the power travels through the switch. A black mark on the end indicates the white wire is hot in this wiring arrangement.

TWO SWITCHES SHARING A HOT WIRE.

Usually two switches in the same room connect to the same circuit so they can share a single hot wire. All the neutral wires are spliced together. Power enters each switch via a pigtail—a short lead—from the black power wire.

THREE-WAY SWITCH WIRING.

Two three-way switches control the same fixture from two different locations. A three-way switch has three terminals (plus the terminal for the ground) and its toggle doesn't have On and Off markings. The hot wire connects to the common terminal, which is usually darker in color than the other terminals. For three-way wiring, see pages 89–91.

Switch and receptacle wiring *(continued)*

MID-RUN RECEPTACLE.

If two cables enter a receptacle box, one brings power to the receptacle and the other leads out to receptacles down the line. This is a mid-run receptacle. The two neutral wires connect to the neutral (silver) terminals, and the two black wires connect to the hot (brass) terminals.

END-RUN RECEPTACLE.

If only one cable enters a receptacle box, the receptacle is at the end of the run. Connect the white wire to the neutral (silver) terminal and the black wire to the hot (brass) terminal.

SPLIT RECEPTACLE.

When two hot wires run to the hot (brass) terminals, and the connecting tab between the two has been broken off, the receptacle is split. Either (1) the receptacle's two outlets are each on a separate circuit so you can plug in two high-amperage appliances without overloading either circuit; or (2) the receptacle is split and switched, meaning one of the outlets is controlled by a wall switch somewhere in the room.

WIRE COLORS.

A different color hot wire designates each circuit in homes that use wires in conduit rather than cable (see pages 152–55). This can help identify the circuit. If, for instance, a device is connected to a blue wire, look for a blue wire in the service panel to find the corresponding circuit breaker. Verify that the breaker does shut off the device before doing any work.

RECEPTACLE THAT BRANCHES OUT.

If three cables enter a box and all the wires connect to the receptacle, then it is a mid-run receptacle that provides power for another branch or fixture. In other words, power leaves the receptacle in two directions. The extra wires should be connected via pigtails; it is not safe to attach two wires to a single terminal.

OTHER WIRING YOU MIGHT FIND

Red and black wires.
Sometimes a single three-wire cable—with a red, black, and white wire—is used to wire two different circuits. The red wire is the hot wire for one circuit, and the black is the hot wire for the other circuit. The white wire is used as a neutral for both circuits.

A receptacle with two hot wires. When two black wires or a black one and a red one connect to the two brass (hot) terminals, the receptacle is split. Either each of its two outlets is connected to a different circuit, or one outlet is controlled by a wall switch and the other is always hot (see page 95).

Wires that travel through. If wires travel through a box but are not connected to the box's device or fixture, they probably are for a different circuit.

With a basic understanding of wiring, you can spot most problems with a home electrical system. The next three pages show some common problems you might find.

If you see a problem, shut off the power to the circuit, test to make sure the electricity is off, and correct the problem before restoring power. If you spot a wiring configuration that you do not understand, call a professional electrician for an evaluation. Do not change or work on any wiring you do not understand.

YOU'LL NEED

TIME: About a day to inspect a modest-size home.

SKILLS: Basic electrical and wiring knowledge.

TOOLS: Voltage tester, screwdriver.

THE POINT OF ATTACHMENT.

Power enters your home either through a weather head, as shown, or an underground cable. Conduct a visual inspection, but do not touch anything. Make sure the wires are firmly secured and the insulation is in good condition. Overhead wires should be high enough to avoid contact. If you see anything that might be a problem, call the electrical utility for an inspection.

OUTDOOR CONNECTIONS.

From the point of entry, cables or conduit travel down your home's siding until they enter the house. The wiring travels through a meter, which may be inside or outside, and then goes to the service panel. All conduits and cables should be solidly attached to the house. The outdoor attachments should be watertight. If the wiring is within reach of children, make sure it is safe. Call the utility if you see any potential problems.

MISSING KNOCKOUT.

Any exposed hole, such as this missing knockout in a basement switch box, is a serious danger. Children or even adults can easily poke a finger in and get a painful shock. Buy a knockout filler, also called a "goof plug" (see page 129), and anchor it firmly to fill the hole.

CRACKED OR MISSING COVERPLATE.

Protect all receptacles and switches with coverplates that are in good condition. If a coverplate is even slightly damaged, replace it.

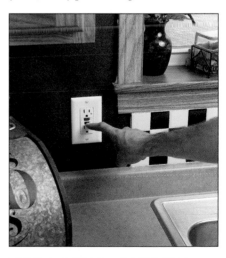

TEST A GFCI RECEPTACLE.

GFCIs (see pages 76–77) do wear out. When that happens a GFCI will supply power but not protection. Test GFCIs every month. When you push the test button, the power should shut off. If not, replace the device.

Inspecting your home's wiring *(continued)*

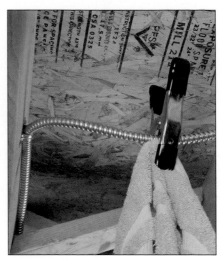

DAMAGED CORD INSULATION.

Cord insulation can become brittle and crack easily, especially if subjected to high heat. Cords are also easy to nick. A repair with electrician's tape is a temporary fix at best. To be safe replace the entire cord. Also replace any cracked or wobbly plugs (see pages 38–43).

MISSING CABLE CLAMP.

Cable clamps protect the cable connection from being pulled apart, help protect the insulation from nicks, and seal the box's hole. An unclamped cable is dangerous. See page 147 for ways to clamp cable.

LOOSE CABLE.

Wherever cable is exposed (typically in a basement, garage, or attic), it should be tightly fastened with straps or staples specifically made for attaching wiring. Unsecured cables are susceptible to damage. And do not use cables as clotheslines or to otherwise support loads.

OVERLOADED RECEPTACLE.

Plugging too many cords into a receptacle poses the risk of overloading a circuit. An arrangement like this also makes it easy to accidentally pull out a plug, and creates a tripping hazard. Install an additional receptacle and move some of the load to other circuits.

BULB TOO BIG.

It's tempting to install a 100-watt bulb in a fixture rated for only 60 watts, but doing so will cause the fixture to overheat dangerously. This may not start a fire, but the extra heat may partially melt insulation and cause it to become brittle. If you need more light, replace the fixture with one that has a higher wattage rating.

BARE BULB IN A CLOSET.

A light bulb, even a low-wattage one, does get hot, which is why modern codes require closet fixtures to have protective globes. If you don't have a globe, at least keep clothing and flammables a minimum of 1 foot away from the bulb. Better yet install a new, safer fixture.

Hot lead attached to neutral terminal.

RECEPTACLE WIRED INCORRECTLY.

Whenever you open a box (see pages 18-19), inspect the wiring. The wire ends should be attached firmly to terminal screws, and the insulation should be free of nicks. On a receptacle the white wire goes to the silver terminal and the black wire connects to the brass terminal.

CROWDED BOX.

If a box contains so many wires that they have to be crammed in, overheating or shorts could result. Try installing an extension ring to enlarge the box. Otherwise replace the box with a larger one.

LOOSE CEILING FIXTURE.

A heavy ceiling fixture, such as a chandelier or a ceiling fan, should be attached to a fan-rated box, which is stronger than a normal ceiling box (see pages 80-81). If the fixture has come loose from the box, it is usually easy to reattach. If the box itself is loose, you may be able to secure it by driving screws into an abutting joist. Otherwise remove the fixture and install a new box.

WRONG BREAKER OR FUSE.

In a service panel, a 14-gauge wire should be connected to a 15-amp breaker or fuse, and a 12-gauge wire should be connected to a 20-amp breaker. If the amperage of a breaker or fuse is too high for the wire, the wiring could overheat dangerously before the breaker trips or the fuse blows. Replace the breaker or the fuse with one of the correct amperage.

UNSAFE WIRE ROUTING.

In a service panel, wires should run neatly around the perimeter inside the box. If wires are bunched together or close to electrical connections, shut off the main breaker or fuse and gently move them to the side. If you see charring or melted insulation, or if the wiring is badly disorganized, call an electrician for an evaluation.

ALUMINUM WIRING

During the early 1970s some homes were built using aluminum wiring. The tendency for aluminum wires to expand when hot and contract as they cool led to loose connections, so aluminum house wiring was discontinued. Aluminum wire is thicker than copper wire (14-gauge aluminum wire is the same diameter as 12-gauge copper wire) and usually has AL printed on the insulation. An aluminum-wired system can be safe, as long as its devices are rated for use with aluminum—they are labeled CO/ALR. If you splice a copper wire to an aluminum wire, be sure to apply antioxidant to the wires, then twist on a wire nut rated for use with aluminum wire. If an aluminum-to-aluminum splice comes loose, do the same.

An older home may have an inadequate and unsafe electrical service. The wiring can be confusing as well. If you are unsure about your home's wiring, have a professional check it out.

Some older systems have only two wires—rather than three—entering the house from the utility company. This arrangement does not have the capacity for the 240-volt circuits needed for ranges, clothes dryers, and other appliances.

Modern residential electrical service provides at least 100 amps of power. This is enough to power a medium-size house with an average number of appliances. If your service panel provides less amperage and you often blow fuses, or if you want to add new circuits, see pages 114–115.

CHECK AN OLD SERVICE ENTRANCE.

A point of attachment like this lacks a modern watertight entrance head (see page 29). Chances are the utility company will install a better attachment if you call them. At least make sure the porcelain insulator is not cracked.

60-AMP FUSE BOX.

A house built in the 1950s or before may have only 60-amp service and a fuse box that contains only four fuses. This small number of circuits limits how many fixtures and appliances you can safely run.

DAMAGED INSULATION.

Old brittle wire insulation can easily crack, and the resulting exposed wire poses a danger. If the problem occurs only in a few spots, shut off the power and wrap the wire with electrician's tape. If much of the wiring is brittle, purchase special shrink-wrap sleeves made for protecting old wires.

DARKENED INSULATION

In some older homes, cloth wire insulation has darkened to the point where you cannot tell a white (neutral) wire from a black (hot) wire. Sometimes this leads to incorrect wiring. If a switch is wired using the neutral wire rather than the hot wire (see page 27), then the switch will turn off the light, but power will still be present in the fixture's box. To be safe flip the switch off and use a voltage detector to check for power in the fixture box.

KNOB-AND-TUBE WIRING.

Some or all of the wiring may be done with individual wires (rather than cable) routed through the framing with ceramic knobs and tubes. This wiring is generally safe if it is correctly installed and protected from damage or contact. But devices usually are not grounded (see page 26), so consider having an electrician rewire the home.

OLDER BOXES.

An old home with plaster ceilings may have pancake ceiling boxes like this. Wires often run through a center pipe, which may have been a gas line once. A box like this is usually not strong enough to hold a heavy fixture such as a ceiling fan. To attach a modern light fixture, you may need to buy special hardware (see pages 80–81).

UNGROUNDED RECEPTACLES.

If an old receptacle has only two slots and no ground hole, it is not grounded. If the receptacle can be grounded (see pages 26 and 48–49), replace it with a three-prong grounded receptacle. Otherwise install a two-prong ungrounded receptacle and do not plug in any appliance that has a three-prong plug.

NONPOLARIZED RECEPTACLE.

A receptacle with two slots the same length is not polarized, which is a hazardous situation (see page 26). Replace it with a polarized receptacle, connecting the neutral wire (white) to the silver terminal and the hot (black) wire to the brass one.

THREE-HOLE ADAPTER.

Use an adapter like this only if it is firmly attached to the mounting screw and the mounting screw is grounded. Test the adapter with a receptacle analyzer to see that it is grounded. If it is not, remove the adapter and use only two-prong plugs. If it is grounded, replace the ungrounded receptacle with a grounded one.

IS THE REST OF THE WIRING SOUND?

In an older home the wiring in boxes may have dangerously brittle insulation, which may make you wonder about all the wiring you cannot see.

As long as the wires are encased in sheathing, you need not lie awake worrying about it. As long as the sheathing is in good shape, the encased wire insulation will last far longer than the insulation that is exposed to the air in boxes.

If your home has wires running through conduit, the wires will be somewhat exposed to the air. Fortunately it is possible to fish new wires through the conduit— a good idea for a system that is more than 60 years old.

Knob-and-tube wiring (above left) with insulation that is generally brittle should definitely be replaced; it is a serious fire hazard.

The electrical service in your house is divided into branch circuits. Each branch circuit supplies power to a particular area of your home. It is important to make sure that no branch circuit carries too great a load, or you will be constantly resetting breakers or replacing fuses. Some appliances need a dedicated separate circuit. An electric stove or clothes dryer, for instance, will have its own 240-volt circuit; other appliances may require their own 120-volt circuits. More often a circuit supplies a number of outlets. Some circuits serve both lights and outlets.

To find out if a circuit is overloaded, add up the total power drawn by the circuit, as outlined below. Check the breaker or fuse to see how many amps the circuit can deliver. If your total use exceeds the amperage the circuit can supply, change your usage. The solution may be as simple as plugging an appliance into a different receptacle—or you may have to add another circuit to your system. For extra safety limit the total load on any circuit to 80 percent of the breaker value—a 16-amp load on a 20-amp breaker, for instance.

Lights ○
Receptacle ⊕

TYPICAL CIRCUIT PLAN.

A well-planned electrical system will have branch circuits that serve easily defined areas or purposes. Unfortunately many homes—especially those remodeled by do-it-yourselfers—have circuits that roam all over the house. Note that some appliances, such as the microwave oven, dishwasher, and disposal, have their own circuits. The electric stove has a separate 240-volt circuit. Otherwise circuits are roughly organized by the rooms they serve and their anticipated demand.

CIRCUIT LOADS

To figure your circuit loads, add up the watts being used. Check the specification label on each appliance. Also note the wattage of the lightbulbs in fixtures on the circuit. Some labels indicate watts as volt-amps (VA). Watts equals volts times amps, so divide the total wattage by 120 (the circuit voltage) to find out how many amperes (amps) the circuit draws when all the appliances and lights are on. This will help you determine whether you are placing too great a demand on a circuit. At right are some typical wattage and amperage figures for common household appliances.

Refrigerator:
500 watts/4.2 amps

Microwave oven:
800 watts/6.7 amps

7,500-BTU air-conditioner:
1,000 watts/8.1 amps

Toaster:
1,050 watts/8.75 amps

Gas dryer:
720 watts/6 amps

Washer:
600 watts/5 amps

Circular saw:
1,200 watts/10 amps

MAPPING YOUR CIRCUITS

When you look inside the door of your service panel, do you see a detailed description of what each branch circuit controls? If not, make a chart. You'll be glad you mapped the circuits the next time you have to turn off a circuit for repairs or improvements or when you have to find a tripped breaker.

Begin by making a map of each floor in the house. Take care to include all receptacles, switches, appliances, and fixtures. Remember that 240-volt receptacles will have their own circuits. You may have to make more than one drawing per floor for a large house.

Have a helper flip switches and test outlets while you stay at the box and write down the findings. If you must work alone, plug in a radio turned to peak volume to find the general area covered by the circuit. The radio will go silent when you switch off the power. Test outlets to find the extent of the circuit.

1 TEST EACH OUTLET.

Mark each circuit breaker or fuse with a number. Turn on all the appliances and lights on one floor. Plug a lamp into every receptacle. Turn off one circuit, and have your helper write the circuit number next to each outlet that went dead.

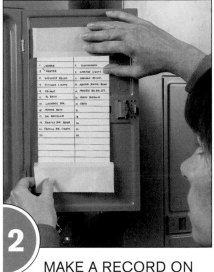

2 MAKE A RECORD ON THE SERVICE PANEL.

Test every circuit for each floor. Write the findings on a sheet of paper and tape it to the inside of the service panel door.

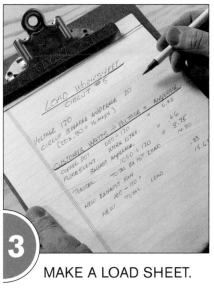

3 MAKE A LOAD SHEET.

To really get a fix on how your house uses electricity, combine the information from circuit mapping with power-use information from appliance labels. Write up a load sheet as shown. It will help you assess capacity for future additions to your electrical system.

CAUTION

HANDLE YOUR SERVICE PANEL WITH RESPECT

Take special care when working around a service panel. Remove cover plates only when you absolutely have to, and replace them as soon as you can. Keep the door shut whenever you are not inspecting the panel—lock it if you think kids may get at it. Remember that even if you have shut off the main power breaker or switch, there is still power entering the box.

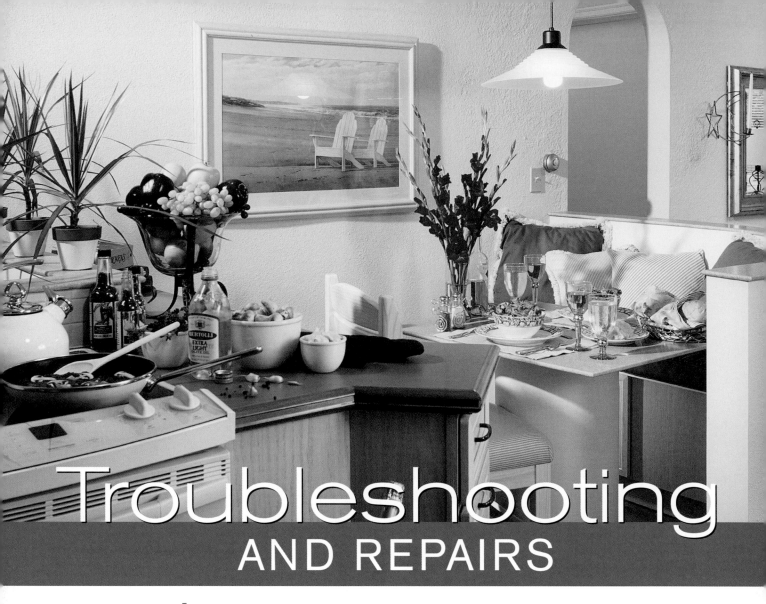

Troubleshooting
AND REPAIRS

In many cases electrical devices and fixtures should be replaced rather than repaired. Switches, receptacles, and even many light fixtures are so inexpensive that it is not worth your while to repair them. Or you may choose to replace a device or fixture simply because you don't like the way it looks.

However, a treasured lamp or an antique chandelier is certainly worth several hours of rewiring work. And in some cases repairing a fixture is actually simpler than replacing it.

Instructions in this chapter walk you through a series of steps. You can attempt a simple fix, then if that does not solve the problem, you can try progressively more serious repairs. If the repair appears to be too involved for you, replace the fixture instead.

Perform all repairs with the power off. Unplug a lamp. Remember to shut off the power to a light fixture not only by flipping off the switch, but also by shutting off the circuit at the service panel.

Many repairs call for the use of a continuity tester (see page 21). This tool lets you know if there is any break along the length of a wire or in a device's circuitry.

A repair is often an occasion to upgrade your service. Consider replacing a defective switch with a dimmer or other special switch (see pages 74–75), or a broken fluorescent fixture with attractive track or Euro-style lighting (see pages 64–67).

MAINTAIN HOME COMFORTS

Keep your home comfortable and cozy by using the techniques in this chapter to maintain pendent fixtures such as the one that illuminates this dining room. This chapter will also provide you with the information to maintain or repair switches and thermostats, such as those found on the far wall of this room.

REPAIR A LAMP

A classy table lamp such as this is certainly well worth repairing, even if you have to replace all the electrical parts.

PRESERVE FIXTURES

Fixtures such as this chandelier and the coordinating wall sconces are often too valuable to discard when they don't work properly. Follow the steps in this chapter to keep them shining brightly.

REPLACING PLUGS AND CORDS

Faulty plugs pose the most common shock and fire hazards in the house. Plugs get stepped on, bumped, and yanked out by their cords. It's a good idea to regularly inspect your plugs—especially old ones—for loose connections, damaged wire insulation, and bent prongs that are in danger of breaking.

Replacing a faulty plug will make your home safer, and the job is easy. Buy a plug that has the same number of prongs as the one you're replacing.

Snap-on plug
20-amp appliance plug
Angle plug
Round-cord plug
Quick-connect plug

Zip cord:
Table lamps, radios

Grounded strand (16-3):
Light extension cords

20-amp, 120-volt (12-3):
Microwave ovens

30-amp, 240-volt (10-3):
Window air-conditioners

TYPES OF PLUGS.

Flat-cord plugs work for lamps, radios, and other low-amperage devices. Round-cord plugs often accommodate thick wire and are used for higher-current appliances such as irons. Newer lamp and extension cord plugs are polarized, with one blade wider than the other (see page 26).

Standard grounded plugs have a third, round prong for grounding; the two flat prongs are polarized.

Appliances that use 240 volts require heavy-duty three-pronged plugs of various configurations.

TYPES OF CORDS.

Cords have stranded, not solid, wire for flexibility. Zip cord, so called because the two wires can be easily zipped apart, is for light-duty appliances and lamps. Use cords with 16-gauge wire for appliances that draw 15 amps or less and 12-gauge wire for 20-amp appliances. For 240-volt appliances, use wire that is 10-gauge or thicker.

YOU'LL NEED

TIME: About ½ hour to replace a plug.

SKILLS: Stripping, tying, and wrapping wire.

TOOLS: Wire stripper, screwdriver, needle-nose pliers.

Replacing a round-cord plug

1 UNDERWRITERS KNOT.

Snip off the old plug. Slide the cord through the body of the replacement plug. Strip off 3 inches of outer insulation and about ½ inch of wire insulation. Tie an Underwriters knot as shown.

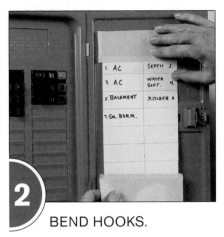

2 BEND HOOKS.

Pull the cord back so the knot is tight to the plug. Twist the wire strands tight with your fingers. Use a pair of needle-nose pliers to shape clockwise hooks to wrap around the screws.

3 CONNECT THE WIRES.

Hook the wires on the screw shanks (attach the black wire to the brass screw), and tighten. Tuck in any stray strands. Make sure all wires and strands are neatly inside the plug. Slip on the cardboard cover.

Repairing a 240-volt plug

1 SLIDE THE PLUG ONTO THE CORD.

A 240-volt plug has a steel clamp that grips the cord, so you don't have to tie an Underwriters knot. Slide the plug onto the cord and strip about ½ inch of insulation from the ends of the three wires. Twist the strands tight, and use needle-nose pliers to form hooks.

2 ATTACH THE WIRES.

Attach the black and red wires to brass-colored terminals, and the white wire to the silver-colored terminal. As you tighten the terminal screws, tuck in any loose strands. Then tuck all the wires in place, tighten the cord clamp, and slip on the cardboard cover.

MAINTAINING AND INSPECTING PLUGS

Electrical plugs carry just as much current as the wiring. They deserve to be treated with respect.

Never remove the grounding prong from an appliance plug. The grounding prong may protect you from shock, especially if the appliance gets wet.

Remove a plug from a receptacle by grasping the plug and pulling straight out. Pulling on the cord may loosen the connections, and pulling at an angle could bend the plug prongs.

If plug prongs do get bent, you can bend them back, but only a finite number of times. Continual bending will cause a prong to eventually crack. If a prong is made of two strips of metal and the strips come apart from each other, you may be able to bend them back together, but you are better off replacing the plug.

Keep a few quick-connect plugs on hand and you'll be less tempted to put off replacing a faulty or questionable plug. Installing one is only slightly more difficult and time-consuming than changing a lightbulb.

Replacing a plug with screw terminals is more like doing actual electrical work, but it takes only a little more time.

YOU'LL NEED

TIME: About 5 minutes to install a quick-connect plug; 15 minutes for a plug with screw terminals.

SKILLS: No special skill required for the quick-connect plug; stripping wire and making connections for the screw-terminal plug.

TOOLS: Knife or scissors for the quick-connect plug; wire stripper, needle-nose pliers, and screwdriver for the screw-terminal plug.

Wiring a quick-connect plug

SCREW-TERMINAL PLUG.

Cut the cord near the old plug. Separate the cord's two wires, and strip ¾ inch of insulation from each wire. Slide the plug cover onto the cord. Twist each wire tight with your fingers, bend it into a hook shape, and firmly attach it to the terminal. Make sure the attachments are firm and remove any loose strands, then slide the plug body up and snap it in place.

NO-STRIP PLUG.

This is the easiest plug to attach. Cut the cord, and do not separate or strip the wires. Slide the plug cover onto the cord. Gently pull apart the plug's prongs, and poke the cord into the hole at the bottom. Squeeze the prongs together, and slide the cover up until it snaps into place.

INSTALLING A SCREW-TERMINAL CORD SWITCH.

To install a rocker cord switch, separate the wires and cut and strip the ends of the hot wire. Strip ¾ inch of insulation from each cut wire end, and twist the bare wires tight. thread the neutral wire through the bottom channel. Connect the stripped wire ends to the terminals, tighten the terminal screws, and replace the cover.

Installing a cord switch

1 SEPARATE THE WIRES, CUT THE HOT ONE.

To install a rotary cord switch, carefully slice through the cord between the two wires, and separate the two wires for about 1½ inches. Snip only the hot (smooth) wire in the middle.

2 LAY THE WIRES IN THE SWITCH SHELL.

Thread the neutral (ribbed) wire through the bottom channel. Thread the two cut ends of the hot (smooth) wire through the upper channel, as shown. Push the wires firmly into place. Replace the cover, and tighten the screw.

Most floor and table lamps consist of a body, a base, a harp to support the shade, and a socket, which holds the lightbulb. The cord usually runs through a hollow threaded rod from the base to the socket.

When a lamp won't work and you know the bulb is OK, check the cord for damage. If the insulation is worn and cracked, replace the entire cord (see page 42). If the cord is OK, the problem is most likely in the socket.

Most lamps have felt bases that must be removed before repairing the lamps. Remove the felt by paring it off with a utility knife. After the repair reapply the felt with white glue.

YOU'LL NEED

TIME: About 1 hour to replace a lamp socket.

SKILLS: Stripping wire, connecting wire to screws.

TOOLS: Wire stripper, screwdriver, needle-nose pliers.

1 PRY UP THE CONTACT.

Unplug the lamp and remove the bulb. Clean out dust or debris in the socket. Scrape rust off the center contact with a flat screwdriver, then gently pry up the tab. If this does not solve the problem, go on to the next two steps to replace the socket.

3 CONNECT THE NEW SOCKET.

Slip the new socket base onto the cord, and tie an Underwriters knot (see page 39). Strip about ½ inch of insulation from the wires, twist the strands tight, and form them into hooks with a pair of needle-nose pliers. Wrap the wires clockwise around the screw shanks and tighten the screws. Reassemble the cardboard insulation and the outer shell. Attach the new socket to the lamp.

2 REMOVE THE SOCKET.

Remove the harp if it is in the way. Examine the socket shell and find the word "press" on the sides. Push hard at that point and pull the unit apart into the components shown. Remove the cord from the socket. Unscrew the socket base from the lamp.

LAMP SOCKET OPTIONS

Replacing a lamp socket allows you to change the way your lamp turns on and off.

■ If the current socket has no switch, you can change to a switched socket—which most people prefer to, say, a cord switch.

■ You can choose either a push-through switch, which turns on and off when you push it from one direction or the other; a rotary switch, which turns on and off when you twist it; or a pull-chain switch.

■ You can also install a socket made for use with a three-way bulb, allowing you to choose one of three light levels.

REWIRING LAMPS

Lamp cords get stepped on and yanked. And if a lamp has a tendency to heat up, the cord's insulation can become cracked near the socket. Replace any cord with damaged insulation; it is dangerous.

Replacing a cord is not difficult. In fact you may want to do it for no other reason than to have a cord that makes a lamp more attractive or to provide a longer cord.

Never work on a lamp or appliance while it is plugged in. Always unplug it first.

1 FEED THE NEW CORD THROUGH.

Disconnect the old cord from the lamp socket and snip off the plug. Tie the new cord to the old one with a piece of string or some tape. Make the connection thin enough that it will slide through the center rod, and pull the new cord through as you withdraw the old one.

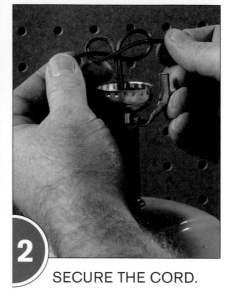

2 SECURE THE CORD.

Snip off the old cord and discard it. Tie an Underwriters knot (see page 39) in the new cord, leaving about 2½ inches of each wire. Strip ½ inch of insulation from each wire.

3 ATTACH THE WIRES.

Twist the strands tight with your fingers. Use needle-nose pliers to form hooks, and wrap them around the terminal screws. Tuck in loose strands as you tighten the terminal screws.

4 REASSEMBLE THE LAMP.

Reassemble the socket and install the harp as shown. Attach a new plug (see pages 38–40). Then put in a bulb, attach the shade, and plug in your lamp.

CAUTION

REPLACE DAMAGED LAMP CORD—DON'T TAPE IT

It may not look dangerous, but nicked and cracked lamp wire insulation is the cause of many fires. And you can receive a painful shock if you touch a bare spot.

If you see a damaged spot and need to keep using the lamp, wrap electrician's tape around the damaged area. But be aware that tape is a temporary solution—it can easily come unwrapped. And if one part of the cord is damaged, chances are other parts are as well. Replace the cord as soon as possible.

CHECKING INCANDESCENT FIXTURES

Though they vary in style, most incandescent fixtures have the same components.

Mounting screws hold a canopy plate against the ceiling. The canopy has one or more sockets for bulbs. A translucent diffuser or globe reduces the glare of bare bulbs. In newer fixtures fiber insulation provides added protection from heat damage to the wires and ceiling. Although it makes installation a bit more difficult, don't remove the fiber insulation.

If a fixture shorts out, causing a circuit to blow and/or creating sparks, the problem is probably in the fixture. If it simply refuses to light, the wall switch may be faulty (see pages 46–47).

YOU'LL NEED

TIME: About ½ hour to inspect a typical fixture.

SKILLS: No special skills needed.

TOOLS: Screwdriver, continuity tester.

1 INSPECT THE SOCKET.

Shut off the circuit that powers the fixture. Inspect the socket. If it is cracked, or if the wires are scorched or melted, replace the socket or the entire fixture. Remove the bulb and check the contact at the socket's base. If it's corroded, scrape the contact with a flat screwdriver or steel wool, and pry it up.

2 CHECK THE WIRING.

If the problem remains, loosen the mounting screws, and drop the fixture from its box. Check for loose connections and damaged wires. Slightly peeling drywall paper or heat-cracked wire insulation means an overheated fixture. Reduce the wattage of the bulbs or replace the fixture. Wrap any bare wires with electrical tape.

CAUTION

USE THE RIGHT BULBS

A label on the fixture lists the maximum bulb wattage allowed. Don't install higher-wattage bulbs. Your fixture will overheat, burn out bulbs quickly, and become dangerous.

Troubleshooting a chandelier

1 TEST THE SOCKETS.

Shut off power to the circuit. Test the sockets of nonworking lights. Attach the continuity tester to the socket's metal threads and touch the probe to the white-wire terminal. The tester should light. Test between the contact in the bottom of the socket and the black-wire terminal.

2 TEST THE WIRES.

Remove the chandelier. You may need to open a junction box where all the wires converge. Determine where all the cords run. To test the wires that run to each socket, clip each wire at the junction box and touch the probe to the inside of the socket.

3 TEST THE STEM WIRES.

Also test the wires that run from the fixture's canopy to the junction box. If you need to replace the wire, tape the new wire to the old one. Then pull out the old wire until the new wire comes through.

TROUBLESHOOTING FLUORESCENT FIXTURES

The heart of an older fluorescent fixture is its ballast, a transformer that steps up voltage and sends it to a pair of lamp holders. The current passes through the lamp holders and excites a gas inside the fluorescent tube, causing its phosphorus-coated inner surface to glow with cool, diffused light.

Compared to incandescent bulbs, fluorescent tubes produce less heat, last longer, and consume less electricity. However, problems with the fixtures sometimes arise. The ballast in a fixture can burn out after years of steady use, and the lamp holders can crack easily if they get bumped. Starters in very old units must be replaced periodically.

1   WIGGLE THE TUBE.

Fluorescent tubes rarely burn out abruptly. If a tube suddenly stops lighting, try wiggling and rotating the ends of the tube to make sure it's properly seated.

2   CHANGE A WORN-OUT TUBE.

A working tube usually has a grayish tinge near its ends. If the ends turn dark gray or black, the tube is failing and should be replaced. Purchase a tube that is the same length and wattage as the old one. If the tube is uniformly dim, it may simply need washing. To wash a tube, remove it from the fixture, wipe it with a damp cloth, and then replace the tube.

3   REPLACE THE STARTER.

Older, delayed-start fluorescent lights flicker momentarily as they light up. If the flickering continues for more than a few seconds, make sure the starter is seated properly. Push it in and turn it clockwise. When the ends of a tube light up but its center does not, the starter is defective. Press the starter in and turn it counterclockwise to remove it.

YOU'LL NEED

TIME: About 1 hour to inspect a fixture and replace a ballast (for example).

SKILLS: No special skills needed.

TOOLS: Screwdriver.

⚠ CAUTION

SAFE DISPOSAL

Never get rid of burned out tubes by breaking them. They contain mercury. Dispose of them whole, or request disposal guidelines.

4 CHANGE THE BALLAST.

If the fixture hums or oozes a tarlike goop, the ballast needs replacing. (Compare prices; you may be better off replacing the entire unit.) To remove the ballast, shut off the power to the fixture, then release the wires at the sockets by pushing a screwdriver into the release openings. Unscrew the ballast and disconnect the wires to the power source. Reassemble with the new ballast.

5 REPLACE A SOCKET.

Take the old socket in to the store to find a replacement that will fit. Strip ¾ inch of insulation from each wire end and poke the wires into the socket's terminal holes.

6 INSPECT THE BOX.

If these steps don't solve the problem, you may not have power going into the fixture. Remove the fixture and look for loose connections and broken or bare wires in the outlet box.

TROUBLESHOOTING FLUORESCENT FIXTURES

Symptom	Solution
Tube does not light.	1. Rotate the tube to make sure it is properly seated. 2. Replace any damaged lamp holders. 3. Replace the starter, if there is one. 4. Check the wall switch and outlet box to see that there is power to the fixture.
Tube flickers or only lights partially.	1. Rotate the tube to make sure it is properly seated. 2. Replace any tubes that are discolored or have damaged pins. 3. Replace the starter, if there is one.
Black substance or humming sound.	1. Replace the ballast or the entire fixture.

After getting flipped thousands of times, a switch can wear out. Unless the problem is a loose wire connection, you usually cannot repair a faulty switch; you'll have to replace it.

Testing and replacing switches is easy. If you want to replace your old switch with something more sophisticated—for example, a dimmer—check out the switch options on pages 122–123.

USE A NEON TESTER ...

Shut off the power, remove the cover plate and the screws holding the switch, and pull the switch out of the box. Turn the switch off and restore power to the circuit. Touch the probes of a neon tester to the switch's screw terminals. If the tester glows, the circuit has power. Turn the switch on. Touch the probes to the terminals again. If the tester glows this time, the switch must be replaced.

OR A CONTINUITY TESTER.

To test a switch using a continuity tester, shut off the power to the circuit leading to the switch and remove the switch from the box. Disconnect all the wires from the switch. Attach the tester clip to one of the terminals and touch the probe to the other. Flip the switch on. The tester will light up if the switch is good. The tester light should go off when you turn the switch off.

SAFE USE OF A CONTINUITY TESTER

Never use a continuity tester on a live circuit. Always shut off the power and disconnect the wires before testing. A battery in the continuity tester sends a small current through the wires to test for a continuous current path from one point to another. The tester is not made to carry household current.

CAUTION

HANDLE WITH CARE

Hold only the metal flanges of the switch when pulling it out of a box. Be careful not to touch the terminal screws or to allow the screws to touch the edge of the box.

TEST A THREE-WAY SWITCH.

To test a three-way switch, remove the switch and attach the clip to the common terminal (it's usually labeled on the switch body). Touch the probe to the other screw terminals; the tester should light when you touch one of them. Flip the switch. The tester should light when you touch the probe to the other terminal.

TEST A SWITCH/RECEPTACLE.

To test a device that has both a switch and a receptacle, attach the continuity tester clip to one of the top (switch) terminals. Touch the probe to the top terminal on the other side. If the switch is working, the tester will light when the switch is on, and not light when it is off.

YOU'LL NEED

TIME: About ½ hour to test and replace a switch.

SKILLS: Using testers (see instructions), connecting wires to screw terminals.

TOOLS: Neon tester, continuity tester, screwdriver.

Replacing switches

1 REMOVE THE OLD SWITCH.

If a switch is damaged, shut off the power to the circuit, remove the screws holding the switch to the box, and gently pull out the device. Loosen the screw terminals and disconnect the wires.

2 ATTACH WIRES TO THE NEW SWITCH.

Inspect the wires in the box, and wrap any damaged insulation with electrical tape. Attach the wires to the terminals of the new switch, and wrap electrical tape around the body of the switch to cover the terminals.

3 REINSTALL THE SWITCH.

Carefully tuck the wires and switch back into the box, and connect the switch to the box by tightening the mounting screws. Don't force anything; switches crack easily.

Replacing a fixture-mounted switch

1 REMOVE THE OLD SWITCH AND TEST THE WIRING.

If a switch on a fixture or lamp does not work, shut off power to the fixture or unplug the lamp. Unscrew the nut holding the switch to the fixture, and pull the switch out. Unscrew the wire nuts and remove the switch's wires, but do not disconnect the other wires from each other. To test a lamp's wiring, plug it in and touch the probes of a voltage tester to the wire ends, as shown. If the tester does not glow, rewire the lamp (see page 42).

2 REPLACE THE SWITCH.

A fixture-mounted switch may operate via a pull chain, a toggle lever, a twist knob, or a pushbutton. All four types fit into the same opening and are interchangeable. Use wire nuts to splice the wire ends of the new switch to the wire ends from the lamp. Insert the switch in the hole, and tighten the nut.

TESTING RECEPTACLES

D amage to receptacles is not always readily apparent. Small cracks can lead to a short, and aged receptacles may not grip plug blades firmly. Receptacles are inexpensive and easy to replace, however, so you can change one for any reason, even if it is just old and worn or the wrong color. If you decide to replace a receptacle with one of a different type—for example, replace an ungrounded receptacle with a grounded one—read pages 26 and 124 first.

YOU'LL NEED

TIME: About 5 minutes to test and 15 minutes to replace a receptacle.

SKILLS: Using a tester (see instructions), connecting wires to terminals.

TOOLS: Neon tester, receptacle analyzer, screwdriver.

1 TEST TO SEE IF THE RECEPTACLE IS LIVE.

With the power to the circuit on, insert one probe of a voltage tester into each slot of the receptacle. Do not touch the metal probes; only touch the insulated wires of the tester. If the tester glows, the receptacle is working. Test both plugs of a duplex receptacle.

2 TEST FOR POWER TO THE BOX.

If the receptacle is not live, check its power source. Shut off the power to the outlet at the service panel, remove the coverplate, disconnect the screws holding the receptacle to the box, and pull out the receptacle. Restore power and touch one probe of the voltage tester to a brass screw terminal and the other to a silver-colored terminal. The tester will light if the receptacle has power.

1 REMOVE THE OLD RECEPTACLE.

Shut off the power to the circuit at the service panel. Note which wires are attached to which terminals. Make notations on pieces of tape and wrap them on the wires if necessary. Loosen the terminal screws and disconnect the wires.

2 WIRE THE NEW RECEPTACLE.

Inspect the wires in the box, and wrap electrical tape around any damaged insulation. Attach the wires to the receptacle, positioning each wire so it hooks clockwise on the terminal screw. Firmly tighten the terminal screws.

3 WRAP WITH TAPE AND INSTALL.

Wrap the body of the receptacle with electrical tape to cover all the terminals. Carefully tuck the wires and the receptacle into the box, and connect the receptacle to the box by tightening the mounting screws. Don't force the receptacle into place—it may crack.

TEST GROUNDING AND POLARIZATION.

Do not turn off the power. Insert one prong of a voltage tester into the short (hot) slot and the other into the grounding hole. The tester will glow if the receptacle is grounded and the slots are polarized. If the tester doesn't glow, put one probe in the grounding hole and the other in the long slot. A glow this time means the hot and neutral wires are reversed. If the tester doesn't glow in either test, the device isn't grounded.

TEST A TWO-SLOT RECEPTACLE.

With the power on, insert one probe of a voltage tester into the short (hot) slot and touch the other probe to the coverplate screw (above). The screw head must be clean and paint-free. Or remove the cover plate and insert one probe in the short slot and touch the other to the metal box (above right). If the neon tester glows, the box is grounded, and you can install a grounded three-hole receptacle.

If the tester doesn't glow, insert one prong into the long (neutral) slot and touch the other to the coverplate screw or the box. A glowing tester means the box is grounded, but the receptacle is not correctly polarized; the hot and neutral wires are reversed. If the tester doesn't glow in either test, the box is not grounded. Do not install a three-hole receptacle.

USING A RECEPTACLE ANALYZER

With this handy device, you can perform a series of tests almost instantly without having to dismantle anything.

Leave the power on, but unplug all equipment and turn off all the switches in the circuit of the receptacle you will be testing. Plug in the analyzer. A combination of glowing lights will tell you what is happening with your receptacle (far right).

ADDING SURGE PROTECTION

Occasionally your electrical service can experience sudden increases in power, known as surges. A surge usually will not harm lights and appliances, but it could damage sensitive electronic equipment, such as a computer.

To protect a few pieces of equipment, buy a surge protector that plugs into an outlet. Or replace an existing receptacle with a surge-protecting receptacle.

Install one the same way you would a normal receptacle. Follow the manufacturer's instructions for connecting the wires on the device to the wires in the wall box.

YOU'LL NEED

TIME: About 15 minutes.

SKILLS: Joining wires.

TOOLS: Screwdriver, wire stripper, lineman's pliers.

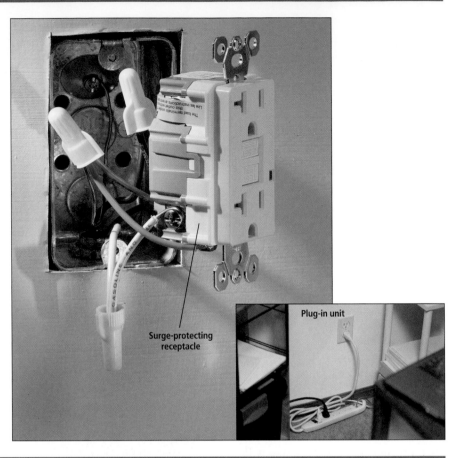

Surge-protecting receptacle

Plug-in unit

ADDING SURGE ARRESTERS TO CIRCUITS

To protect a circuit against surges, install a surge arrester in your service panel. At the service panel, shut off the main circuit breaker, and take off the panel cover. Remove the ½-inch knockout nearest to the circuit you want to protect. Insert the surge arrester through the knockout hole and fix it in place by tightening the nut. Cut the wires as short as possible for maximum protection. Attach the white wire to the neutral bus bar and the black wire(s) to breakers.

YOU'LL NEED

TIME: About 1 hour.

SKILLS: Understanding of your service panel.

TOOLS: Screwdriver, tongue-and-groove pliers, wire stripper.

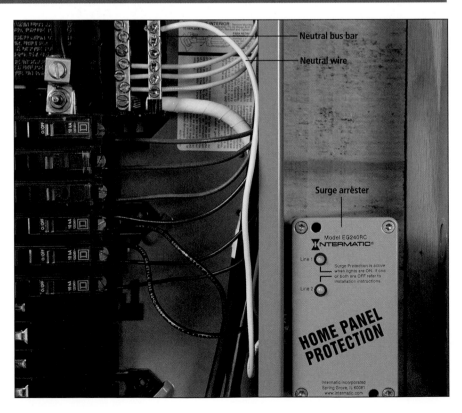

Neutral bus bar

Neutral wire

Surge arrester

Model EG240RC
INTERMATIC

HOME PANEL PROTECTION

TROUBLESHOOTING CIRCUIT BREAKERS

Think of a circuit breaker as a heat-sensing switch. As the illustrations, right, show, when the toggle is on, current flows through a set of contacts attached to a spring and lever. The contacts are held together by tension in the bimetal strip through which the current flows.

If there is a short or an overload in the circuit, the bimetal strip heats up and bends. As it bends it releases a lever that opens the spring-loaded contact. The contact remains open until the toggle is manually reset.

ANATOMY OF A CIRCUIT BREAKER

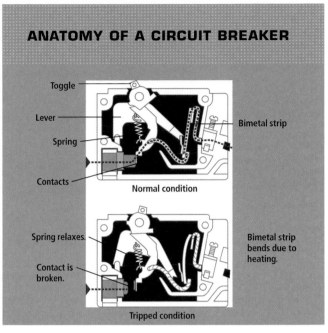

Toggle
Lever
Spring
Bimetal strip
Contacts
Normal condition

Spring relaxes.
Contact is broken.
Bimetal strip bends due to heating.
Tripped condition

YOU'LL NEED

TIME: A few seconds to reset a breaker; about 10 minutes per device to inspect for shorts.

SKILLS: No special skills needed.

TOOLS: Screwdriver.

IDENTIFY A TRIPPED BREAKER.

A tripped breaker is recognizable in any of the four ways shown at right. To find out whether the problem has corrected itself, reset the breaker. If the problem persists, the breaker will shut itself off again. Usually the problem is an overload, and you only need to unplug or turn off one of the circuit's big energy users. If the circuit breaker keeps tripping even though it isn't overloaded, suspect a short. A defective plug, cord, or socket may be the problem.

Tripped breakers and how to reset them

Tripped position: center to reset, flip off, then on

Tripped position: off to reset, flip to on

Tripped position: red flag showing, switch in center to reset, flip off, then on

Tripped position: off to reset, press in and release

Wire pulled loose

Frayed insulation

CHECK CONNECTIONS IN BOXES.

Short circuits can occur in electrical boxes. Look for a loose wire that has shorted out against the box.

INSPECT WIRING.

Frayed or nicked insulation will expose wire and could cause a short. Wrap damaged insulation with layers of electrical tape.

WATCH FOR OVERHEATED FIXTURES.

Heat can damage wire insulation and sockets. Never use bulbs with higher wattage ratings than recommended for the fixture.

TROUBLESHOOTING FUSES

Fuses serve the same purpose as circuit breakers. Instead of switching off the current as a breaker does, though, a fuse contains a strip of metal that melts when too much current flows in the circuit. When this happens, you must eliminate the short or overload (see page 51) and replace the blown fuse.

Solder-filled base takes a few seconds to melt and shut down the circuit.

Time-delay fuse

Tamperproof fuse

Spring-loaded tab prevents adapter from being unscrewed.

YOU'LL NEED

TIME: 10 minutes to inspect your fuses.

SKILLS: Using continuity tester.

TOOLS: Continuity tester, fuse puller.

Normal unblown fuse

Shorted fuse

Overloaded fuse

UNDERSTANDING BLOWN FUSES.

By examining a fuse you usually can tell what made it blow—an overload or a short. A short circuit usually explodes the strip, blackening the fuse window. An overload usually melts it, leaving the window clear.

FUSE OPTIONS.

A tamperproof fuse is an important safety device that makes it impossible to install a fuse with a higher amperage rating than the circuit is designed for. Its threaded adapter fits permanently into the fuse socket and accepts only a fuse with the proper rating.

When an electric motor on a washing machine or refrigerator starts up, it causes a momentary overload, which can blow fuses unnecessarily. A time-delay fuse avoids this problem—only a sustained overload will blow the fuse, not a brief surge.

Ferrule-contact cartridge fuse

Knife-blade-contact cartridge fuse

Fuse puller

CARTRIDGE FUSES.

Ferrule-contact cartridge fuses handle 30- to 60-amp circuits. Knife-blade-contact fuses carry 70 amps or more. Handle both with extreme caution. Touching either in a live circuit with your bare hand could fatally shock you.

REMOVING A CARTRIDGE FUSE.

For safety keep a plastic fuse puller with your spare fuses and use it as shown. Note, too, that the ends of a cartridge fuse get hot, so don't touch them immediately after you've pulled the fuse.

TESTING A CARTRIDGE FUSE.

To see if a cartridge fuse has blown, check it with a continuity tester. Clamp or hold the clip on one end, and touch the probe to the other. The bulb will light if the fuse is good.

A doorbell system incorporates a transformer, which reduces 120-volt line current to between 6 and 30 volts. Light-gauge wire (bell wire) connects the low-voltage side of the transformer to the bell, chime, or buzzer and a doorbell button in a circuit. Pressing the button, which is a spring-loaded switch, closes the circuit and activates the bell, chime, or buzzer.

If your bell does not work, find the cause by using the process of elimination described in the steps below and on pages 54–55. A voltmeter or multitester will make the job easier, but you also can do most tests with a short piece of bell wire or a screwdriver.

Unless you are working on the transformer, there's no need to shut off the power while inspecting a doorbell. The current from the transformer is not hazardous.

YOU'LL NEED

TIME: You may find and solve the problem in minutes, or it could take several hours.

SKILLS: Using a continuity tester, perhaps a multitester.

TOOLS: Screwdriver, continuity tester, multitester, short piece of wire.

Single-button system

120 volts

Low-voltage transformer

Button

Chime

Two-button system

120 volts

Low-voltage transformer

Rear

Front

Chime

Rear Button

Front Button

CHECK WIRES TO THE BUTTON.

To check a doorbell system, remove the button, turn it over, and examine the connections. To make sure that the wires cannot accidentally slip back through the hole, attach a spring clip. Scrape away any corrosion on the terminals. Tighten the connections to the terminals. Wrap any faulty insulation with electrical tape.

Clip keeps wires from slipping into hole.

Terminals

Repairing or replacing doorbells *(continued)*

Jump across terminals with a wire or screwdriver.

2

TEST THE BUTTON BY JUMPING …

Weather and abuse make buttons the most vulnerable parts of a bell system. Test a button by jumping its terminals with a short piece of bell wire as shown. If the bell sounds, the button is faulty and should be replaced.

OR USING A CONTINUITY TESTER.

You can also test the button by disconnecting the wires and touching both terminals with a continuity tester. If the tester glows when the button is pressed, the button is working. If the bell still doesn't sound, disconnect the button, twist its wires together, and test further.

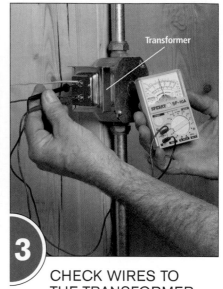

Transformer

3

CHECK WIRES TO THE TRANSFORMER.

Find your transformer. It may be near your home's service panel or attached to a junction box in the vicinity of the door or the bell. Look for corrosion, loose wires, or faulty insulation.

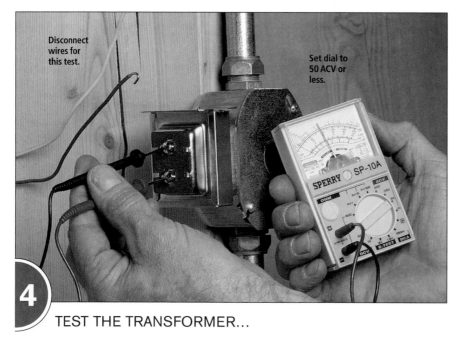

Disconnect wires for this test.

Set dial to 50 ACV or less.

4

TEST THE TRANSFORMER…

To check the transformer, disconnect both wires and touch each terminal with the probes of a voltmeter or multitester. Set the dial at 50 ACV. If the meter shows no current at all, the transformer is the culprit and should be replaced. You also can test a transformer by jumping the low-voltage terminals with a screwdriver. If you see a weak spark, it is OK.

AND REPLACE IF NECESSARY.

Shut off the power. Take off the coverplate of the electrical box, remove the transformer, and disconnect the wires. Wire the new transformer just like the old one, and reassemble the bell.

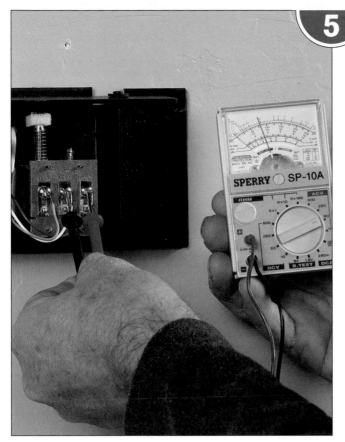

5 INSPECT THE BELL.

If the button, the wires, and the transformer are not to blame, check the bell. Remove the cover. Look for loose or broken connections. Even if you don't have a second button, the chime will have terminals labeled front and rear. Touch the voltmeter or multitester probes to the front and trans (meaning "transformer") terminals. If the meter registers a reading, then power is going to the bell, but the bell is defective. If you have a rear button, test again, touching the rear and trans terminals.

If you don't have a voltmeter, test the bell by removing it and temporarily wiring it directly to the transformer. If it is working, it will ring.

IF EVERYTHING IS OK, IT'S THE WIRES

If the button, transformer, and chimes check out, then the trouble is probably a broken wire. Disconnect wires going into the bell, and test the current flow with a voltmeter or multitester. Or touch the front and rear wires to the transformer wire, and look for a spark.

REPLACING CHIME UNITS

When shopping for a doorbell, consider your wall: Will the new unit cover up the discolored area left by the old one, or will it require you to do some touch-up painting? Also make sure the doorbell you choose has the same voltage rating as its transformer.

INSTALL A REMOTE-CONTROLLED CHIME

Running new wires is a time-consuming job. If you have damaged wires, consider installing a remote-controlled bell. This will cost more than a regular unit, but it saves you the trouble of running wires.

1 LABEL WIRES AND REMOVE THE CHIME.

You can shut off power to the circuit, but it's not necessary because the voltage is so low. The terminals are labeled, so mark the wires accordingly as you disconnect them. These labels also will prevent the wires from accidentally slipping through the hole and into the wall. Unscrew the chime from the wall, and remove it.

2 INSTALL THE NEW CHIME.

Attach the new chime to the wall with mounting screws. Use plastic anchors if you cannot drive a screw into a stud. Connect the low-voltage wires to the terminals, and attach the cover.

A thermostat is a switch that senses temperature and turns your heater or air-conditioner on and off. Most homes have low-voltage units like the one described here. A transformer reduces power from 120 volts to around 24 volts and sends it to the thermostat. Some systems have two transformers, one for heating and one for air-conditioning.

Possible causes of thermostat problems include faulty wiring, corroded thermostat contacts, and a defective transformer.

YOU'LL NEED

TIME: About 1 hour for most inspections and repairs.

SKILLS: No special skills needed.

TOOLS: Voltmeter or multi-tester, continuity tester, screwdriver, artist's brush, short piece of wire.

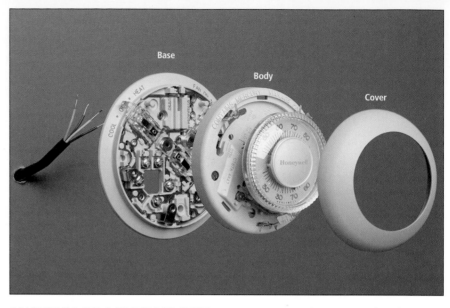

Base   Body   Cover

ANATOMY OF A THERMOSTAT.

A low-voltage system begins with a transformer either mounted to a panel on the furnace or connected to an electrical box. Anywhere from two to six thin wires (depending on how many items are being controlled) lead to the thermostat base, where they are connected to terminals. The thermostat body contains the heat-sensing device and the control dial. Because the voltage is so low, it is not necessary to shut off power to the thermostat while working on it—unless you are working on the transformer.

Coverplate removed

1

CLEAN THE THERMOSTAT.

Dust can cause a thermostat to malfunction. Remove the coverplate and brush out the thermostat with an artist's brush. Pay special attention to dust and dirt on contacts.

2

REMOVE THE BODY.

Remove the screws that hold the thermostat body to the base, and pull the body away. Check to see that the base is fastened to the wall. If it is loose, the thermostat could tilt, possibly affecting the settings. Blow on the body to remove more dust, but do not handle the parts inside—they are sensitive.

3

INSPECT THE BASE CONNECTIONS.

Look for loose, corroded, or broken wires coming into the base. If any are damaged, clip them, strip insulation from the ends, and reattach them. Tighten all the terminal screws to make sure the connections are secure.

Terminals will be marked with letters as shown.

Though marked "Y" a blue wire usually is attached here.

G

R

W Y

4

HOT-WIRE THE TERMINALS.

Cut a short piece of wire and strip insulation from both ends. Use it to jump between terminals. Touch one end to the R terminal and one to W, and the heater's burner should come on. Touch Y and G, and the fan should come on. If they do not, the thermostat is faulty and should be replaced.

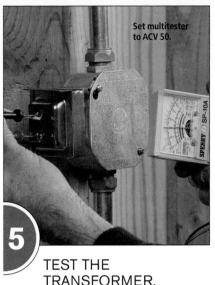

Set multitester to ACV 50.

5

TEST THE TRANSFORMER.

If the thermostat checks out, test the transformer. Touch one probe of a voltmeter or multitester to each of the low-voltage terminals on the transformer. Set the dial to 50 ACV. If the meter does not detect current, the transformer is defective and needs to be replaced.

6

CHECK POWER TO THE TRANSFORMER.

Before you buy a new transformer, open up the transformer box and make sure that there is power leading to the transformer. Touch one probe of a neon tester to the hot wires and the other to the box (if grounded) or the neutral wires.

INSTALLING A PROGRAMMABLE THERMOSTAT.

A programmable thermostat automatically changes the temperature in your home for sleeping and waking hours. It also can deliver different temperatures when you're away.

There are many options to choose from. Some control heat only while others also control air-conditioning. Some can be completely programmed in one sitting; others require a week-long run-through.

When shopping for a new thermostat, know the brand name and model number of your old thermostat and the heating and air-conditioning units to

make sure the new thermostat is compatible. Here are the general guidelines for installation, but make sure to follow the manufacturer's instructions that come with the unit.

9814

REMOVAL AND INSTALLATION

Label the wires as you remove them from the old thermostat. Take off the old thermostat. Pull the wires through the new wall plate, and mount the plate securely to the wall. Check that it is level. Push any excess wire back into the wall and hook up the wires according to the manufacturer's instructions.

Attach the body to the coverplate. Set the clock and program the unit according to the manufacturer's instructions. Attach the cover.

Wiring
IMPROVEMENTS

This chapter shows the most popular and cost-effective improvements you can make to your electrical system. It starts with the simplest of tasks—changing lightbulbs—and progresses to major installations you may want done by a professional electrician. You'll find many upgrades well within your capabilities. Step-by-step instructions help guide you through the process so you can feel confident about the safety and durability of your work.

Always remember this key rule: Unless you are working with a low-voltage installation, such as a thermostat or door chime, always shut off the power and test to be sure the power is absent before you begin work on these projects.

Fortunately old and new electrical boxes are standard sizes, so you can usually fit a new device or fixture onto an old box or hardware. In some cases you may need to buy special hardware to make a new fixture fit onto an older system, but these parts are readily available.

Before installing new lighting, consult the front pages of this book for decorating ideas and practical tips.

DINING LIGHT

You can replace an existing ceiling fixture with a pendent light such as this one in a few hours. If you have to run cable and install boxes for the fixture and a switch, the job could take a full day, plus you will likely need to patch holes in the ceiling and walls.

LIGHT FOR READING

Don't neglect the simplest improvement of all to your electrical system-- buying and plugging in a great-looking lamp.

ENHANCE WALL DISPLAYS

Though it looks complicated, track lighting is relatively quick to install, as long as there is an existing ceiling fixture.

CHANGING LIGHTBULBS

It takes only one do-it-yourselfer to change a lightbulb. Changing a lightbulb is usually easy, but choosing the right replacement bulb calls for some thought.

Check the label on the lamp or light fixture that shows the wattage limit for bulbs. If you install a standard bulb of a higher wattage than recommended, the fixture or lamp will overheat. This probably will not start an immediate fire, but it will likely damage the wire insulation or light sockets, possibly causing problems later. If you need more illumination, consider a screw-in fluorescent or a halogen bulb, each of which delivers more light for less wattage. Or install a new fixture.

LIGHTBULBS TO CHOOSE

Standard incandescent bulbs cost the least and certainly do the job. Bulbs labeled "long life" will more than pay for themselves. However, incandescents are not very energy efficient. Consider purchasing fluorescents that can be screwed into regular sockets. They will last longer and use far less energy. Most take a few seconds to become bright. If that is a problem, consider a halogen bulb, which is nearly as energy efficient but lights up immediately.

Most household fixtures and lamps take a standard lightbulb with a medium base. Decorative fixtures or lamps may require bulbs with different-size bases.

For track and recessed lighting, choose a flood bulb for wide illumination or a spot bulb when you want to highlight a small area.

Halogen fixtures use low voltage, and only halogen bulbs will work in them. Flood and spot bulbs are available for halogens. Be aware that halogen bulbs get very hot.

Decorative incandescents

Appliance bulb

Halogens

Spotlights

Candelabra base incandescents

Three-way with large base

Screw-in fluorescents

Sodium

Metal halide

Incandescent with standard base

Flood lights

CHECK A BULB.

If a light fixture or lamp suddenly stops lighting, you probably just need to change the bulb. First try screwing it in; it may be loose. If a bulb flickers even when screwed in tight, the light fixture may have a loose wire connection. Unscrew the bulb, hold it next to your ear, and jiggle it. A burned-out bulb usually tinkles audibly.

REMOVING A BROKEN BULB.

If a bulb is broken, shut off the power to the circuit. Depending on how much of the glass envelope remains, you may be able to grip the bulb by inserting a broom handle or other piece of wood into the center.

POTATO TRICK.

If a broomstick does not do the job, try jabbing the broken shards with a potato. After unscrewing throw away the potato and the bulb base.

FLUORESCENT TUBE OPTIONS.

Fluorescent lighting doesn't need to feel cold and industrial. At a home center you will find a variety of fluorescent lighting choices, ranging from the coldest (and cheapest) to the very warm. Tubes labeled "full spectrum" or "daylight" deliver illumination similar to the sun's. Grow-light tubes mimic the sun even more closely, providing light that helps indoor plants thrive.

Dramatically change the appearance of a room by adding or replacing a ceiling light. Although there are many choices, from plain ceiling fixtures to elaborate chandeliers, all install in essentially the same way: Power is drawn from a ceiling-mounted box designed to support a particular fixture. If you are replacing a ceiling fixture, take the time to inspect the wires and the area around the outlet box for heat damage (see page 30).

YOU'LL NEED

TIME: 1 hour to mount a simple fixture; more time is needed for elaborate units.

SKILLS: Basic carpentry and wiring skills.

TOOLS: Screwdriver, pliers.

1 REMOVE A FLUSH-MOUNTED FIXTURE.

Shut off the power. Remove the globe or diffuser and the bulbs. Then remove the screws or the cap nut holding the canopy in place, and drop the fixture down. Disconnect the black and white wires. Check the wires for cracks in the insulation. To replace the wire, see page 43.

2 INSTALL A NEW STRAP.

The box may already be equipped with mounting hardware compatible with your new fixture. If not, install a new strap. Some ceiling fixtures come with a strap and may have other mounting hardware.

3 WIRE THE FIXTURE.

Support the fixture with a bent coat hanger so both hands are free to do the wiring. Connect the ground wire either to the box's ground wire or to the box itself (see page 139). Splice the fixture's white lead to the box's white wire and the black lead to the black or colored wire, and twist on wire nuts (see pages 136–138).

4 MOUNT THE CANOPY.

Carefully tuck the wires into the box, and push the canopy into position. If the canopy mounts with two screws, start each of them into the holes in the strap. Check again that the wires are all tucked away, and tighten the screws. If the fixture mounts with a center nut, see the instructions on the opposite page.

5 ADD THE GLOBE.

Make sure the setscrews (there are usually three) are just started into the threaded holes in the side of the canopy; they should not protrude in yet. Push the globe into the canopy's lip, check that it is all the way up, and gently tighten the setscrews.

Installing a pendant light

1 INSTALL A NIPPLE.

Shut off the power. Remove the old fixture (see page 62). Install a strap that has a threaded center hole, if necessary. Screw a nipple (a short length of threaded tubing) into the strap so it hangs down far enough to mount the pendent light's canopy.

2 WIRE THE LIGHT.

If the light has a chain, remove links as needed so the light will hang at the desired height. Check to see if the canopy will fit (next step). Thread wires up through the chain, and cut them to length so they will fit comfortably in the box. Connect the ground wire. Splice the neutral (ribbed) wire to the box's white wire and the hot wire to the box's black or colored wire.

3 ATTACH THE CANOPY.

Restore the power and test the light. Turn the power off again. Carefully tuck the wires into the box, slide the canopy up, and tighten the mounting nut onto the nipple.

INSTALLING A LIGHT WITH A CENTER STUD.

If a fixture's canopy has a single hole in the middle, it mounts using a fixture stud or a nipple. The stud or nipple pokes through the canopy just far enough to attach the nut. Cut the stud rather than screwing it deep into the box, which could damage the wiring. Splice and tuck the wires into the box, slide the canopy over the stud, and screw on the mounting nut.

CEILING LIGHT WITH SWIVEL STRAP.

If you need to rotate the fixture for a good appearance, install a swivel strap. Wire and mount as you would a standard fixture, but hold off the final tightening until you are certain of the fixture's alignment.

MEDALLIONS.

If your ceiling is damaged around the ceiling box, a fixture with a wide canopy may cover up the imperfections. To cover a larger area, or for a decorative touch, install a medallion. Most come with double-sided tape, which holds them temporarily in place while you install the light.

Track lighting offers a lot of flexibility. After it is installed, you can easily change the type and number of lights, their positions, or the direction they aim.

The initial hookup is similar to other ceiling fixtures (see page 62). Installing the tracks, though, so they are properly aligned in your room involves measuring your ceiling and establishing lines for correct placement. Have two ladders and one helper on hand for placement. (If you do not have an existing box to connect into, see pages 134–135.)

YOU'LL NEED

TIME: 4 to 6 hours for a 12-foot system if you are working from an existing ceiling box.

SKILLS: Connecting wires in a box, attaching to a ceiling.

TOOLS: Tape measure, phillips screwdriver, drill with screwdriver bit.

Ceiling electrical box
Mounting plate
Track
Light unit
Canopy

HOW TRACK LIGHTING GOES TOGETHER.

Instructions for your lighting equipment will tell you specifically how to make connections. Most track lights go together in the following way: A mounting plate connects to the ceiling electrical box and transfers power to metal contact strips inside the track; a canopy covers the connections. Each light unit has two contacts at the base. These conduct power to the light from the electrified contact strips in the track. Most units pivot so they can highlight a specific area.

① WIRE THE MOUNTING PLATE.

Shut off the power. Remove the existing light. Connect the plate's ground wire (see page 139). Following the manufacturer's instructions, connect the mounting-plate leads or terminals to the box wires—white to white and black to black or colored (see pages 136–138).

② ATTACH THE MOUNTING PLATE.

Tuck the wires carefully into the box, push the mounting plate into position, and drive screws into the box's strap. Locate joists with a stud finder, and determine how you will attach the track (Step 5).

③ ADD THE TRACK.

Cut the track or tracks to the desired length using a hacksaw. While a helper holds the other end, position the track on the mounting plate and attach it with screws.

4 MEASURE FOR TRACK ALIGNMENT.

While your helper continues to hold the track, measure out from the wall and position the track so it is parallel to the wall.

5 CONNECT THE TRACK TO THE CEILING.

If the track runs across joists, drive mounting screws through the track and into the joists. If the track runs parallel to the joists, drill holes approximately every foot, tap in plastic anchors, and drive screws into the anchors.

6 TURN A CORNER.

When your setup includes an angle, snap a 90-degree elbow onto the end of the track you just installed. While a helper holds the other end, slide the new track onto the elbow. Attach the new track as you did the first. Cover all open ends.

7 ATTACH THE LIVE-END CONNECTOR.

The mounting plate has a connector that makes an electrical connection with the track. Push the connector into the track and twist it so it seats firmly. Snap the canopy over the connector.

8 INSTALL THE LIGHTS.

Some track lights are screwed onto the track using a metal arm. Others, as shown, simply twist on. Position the lights where desired, restore power, and test. Move the lights or rotate them to achieve the illumination you desire.

TRACK LIGHTING OPTIONS

You can run track lighting in just about any configuration. In addition to the L fitting shown in Step 6, you can buy a flexible fitting that can make a turn of any angle; a T fitting for branching out in one direction; or a cross-shape fitting for branching out in two directions.

Track lights (lamps) are available in a variety of styles. You can install several types of lights on the same track to suit different purposes—for instance, you could have several floodlights illuminating walls with one spotlight shining on a work of art or a cabinet full of glassware.

HANGING EURO-STYLE LIGHTS

This is an inexpensive way to add a decorative touch. Similar to track lighting, this system allows you to move and reorient the individual lights.

The basic installation is straightforward. However, expect to spend some time planning the route of the track. You may want to hold the track up against the ceiling in various configurations to determine which arrangement works best.

Several styles are available. Some feature a track that can be bent into curves; others have rigid tandem poles; and others have twin wires. In each case individual lights hang from the tracks or wires.

A transformer located in the canopy reduces power to about 12 volts, so the electrical parts are not dangerous once installed and turned on. However, the basic connection uses standard household current, so be sure to shut off the power before installation.

1 INSTALL THE MOUNTING HARDWARE.

Shut off the power. Remove the existing ceiling fixture, or run power to a new ceiling box (see pages 86–87). Install the strap and the stud (short threaded rod) that comes with the light.

2 WIRE THE MOUNTING PLATE.

In this model three fixture leads connect to the house wires, and three others connect to the canopy. Thread the wires for the canopy through the hole so they protrude downward. Connect the other ground wire (see page 139). Splice the white lead to the box's white wire and the black lead to the black or colored wire (see pages 136–137).

YOU'LL NEED

TIME: 2 to 3 hours once you've decided on the layout.

SKILLS: Connecting wires in a box, measuring, and installing hardware.

TOOLS: Tape measure, lineman's pliers, wire stripper, drill with screwdriver bit, screwdriver.

3 ATTACH THE MOUNTING PLATE.

Tuck the wires into the box, and thread the mounting plate over the stud and up against the box. Add the washer and nut, and tighten the nut.

4 WIRE AND ATTACH THE CANOPY.

Connect the leads to the terminals on the canopy. Push the canopy up onto the mounting plate, and twist it to lock it in place. Add side screws to hold it firm.

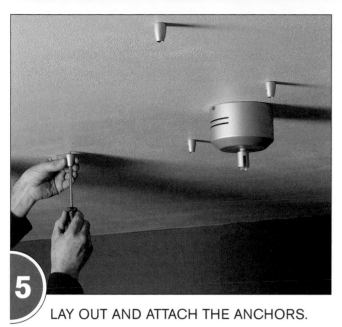

5 LAY OUT AND ATTACH THE ANCHORS.

Determine the path you want the track to follow on your ceiling, and make light pencil marks indicating where the anchors will go. Keep the anchors evenly spaced. At each location drill a hole, tap in a plastic anchor, and attach it by driving a screw.

6 CONNECT THE TRACK.

Insert a rod into each anchor, and tighten a setscrew to hold it firm. Working with a helper, push the track into all the rods. Screw on a cap at each rod, but do not tighten. Reexamine the layout, adjust the track if needed, then tighten the caps.

7 ATTACH THE LIGHTS.

Slip each light's base up onto the track, and screw on the cap. When the lights are arranged as you like, tighten the caps.

ANOTHER TYPE OF LIGHT

Some Euro lights dangle from two wires. Keep a light like this out of the reach of small children to avoid accidents. The wires are actually hot when the light is turned on, although they are not dangerous because they carry only low voltage. A canopy containing a transformer hooks to the ceiling fixture and connects to the wires via wires of the same type.

Recessed fixtures are a good choice if you need plenty of light but don't want it to stand out visually. Because each fixture has its own integral electrical box, there is no need to install electrical boxes, making this the easiest way to add new (as opposed to replacement) lighting.

If you are installing multiple recessed lights, plan the layout on a piece of graph paper. Be aware, however, that whenever you run into a joist—which happens fairly often—you will have to move the light over several inches.

CAUTION

KEEP IT COOL

A recessed light can build up a lot of heat, which can lead to ceiling damage, melted wire insulation, and possibly fire. If insulation will come within 3 inches of a recessed light, you must install a fixture rated insulated compatible (IC). If you install non-IC fixtures, keep them at least 3 inches away from insulation, and don't place them in a cramped space. Use bulbs of the recommended type and wattage. Don't leave flammable materials, such as scraps of insulation paper, near the fixture.

YOU'LL NEED

TIME: About 3 hours to install four lights, after running the cable from the switch.

SKILLS: Cutting a clean hole in the ceiling, running cable through joists, attaching wires.

TOOLS: Keyhole saw, drywall saw, screwdriver, drill with screwdriver bit, fish tape, fishing drill bit, lineman's pliers, wire stripper.

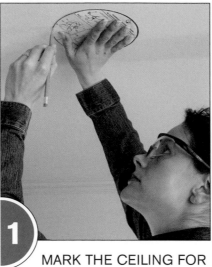

1 MARK THE CEILING FOR A HOLE.

Mark the centers of all the planned lights. Use a stud finder or drill a hole and insert a bent wire to check for nearby joists, adjusting the hole positions if needed. Place the fixture's cardboard template on the ceiling and trace the cut line.

3 FISH CABLE TO THE HOLE.

For tips on fishing cable, see pages 140–146. If you are running cable perpendicular to the joists, drill a hole in a nearby joist. Then cut access holes and drill holes in the other joists that you must cross. Using a fishing bit on a drill can eliminate the need for some access holes.

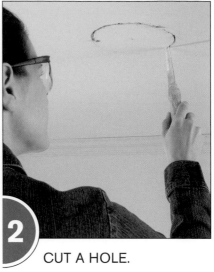

2 CUT A HOLE.

Use a drywall saw to cut a hole in the drywall. If the ceiling is plaster, cutting will be more difficult. Start with a knife, then switch to a keyhole saw, taking care not to vibrate the lath, which can cause the plaster to crack.

4 WIRE THE LIGHT.

Strip the sheathing and wire ends. Connect the ground wires, and splice the white lead to the white wire(s) and the black lead to the black or colored wire(s). Tuck the wires into the fixture's junction box, and close the cover.

5 THREAD THE CAN INTO THE HOLE.

Position the can's mounting clips so they will not get in the way. Carefully insert the cables and the junction box up into the hole. Then push the can up so its lip is against the ceiling.

6 ANCHOR THE FIXTURE.

The fixture grasps the ceiling drywall or plaster via three clips. Use a screwdriver to push up on the clip, which causes the part outside the box to move downward. Each clip should click into place.

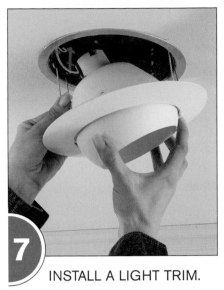

7 INSTALL A LIGHT TRIM.

Various trim options are available. The type shown connects via two pairs of spring hooks. Squeeze one pair, insert the ends into the can's holes, and let go. Repeat with the other pair. Push the trim up until it snaps into place. Other trims connect via coiled springs, which also attach to holes inside the can.

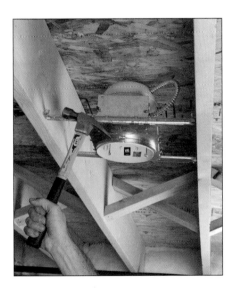

INSTALLING A NEW-WORK FIXTURE.

If the joists are exposed, install a light designed for new construction. Slide the mounting bars outward and fasten each to the joist with a nail or screw. Then slide the can to adjust its position.

Wall washer   Swiveling eyeball   Reflector

Watertight lens   Open (exposed bulb)   Black baffle

TRIM OPTIONS.

An eyeball trim can be swiveled to point at a feature on the wall or a tabletop. A reflector trim increases the brightness of the light. Use a wall washer trim to highlight a section of the wall. If you are installing lights in a damp location, use a trim with a watertight lens.

ADDING WALL SCONCES

Wall sconces are ideal for hallways, stairways, and any room that needs indirect accent lighting. Installing a wall sconce is similar to adding a new light fixture. The only difference is the location and type of fixture box used. As with ceiling lights, you can control as many lights as you want with one switch. You can control one or more lights from two different locations by using three-way switches. See pages 88–93 for the various options.

Ideally you want to secure the fixture box to a framing member as well as the drywall or plaster. Use one of the standard retrofit boxes.

YOU'LL NEED

TIME: About a full day to install a new switch and two sconces, not including any wall patching.

SKILLS: Basic electrical skills, plus cutting and patching walls.

TOOLS: Keyhole saw, screwdriver, lineman's pliers, drill, fish tape.

1 CUT HOLES AND RUN CABLE.

Shut off the power. Find a junction box or a receptacle with power you can use. Cut a vertical hole for the switch box and horizontal or round holes for the sconce boxes (see page 134). Run cable from the power source to the switch and from the switch to the holes (see pages 140–147). Fasten cable to the boxes, allowing an extra 8 inches of cable to protrude at each box. Attach the boxes to the walls.

2 WIRE THE SCONCES.

Strip the sheathing and the wire insulation, then make the electrical connections (see pages 136–139). Note that wires travel both into and out of the first sconce fixture box. Wire the switch (see page 87).

3 INSTALL THE SCONCES.

Tuck the wires into the box, screw a mounting strap to the box, and attach the sconce to the mounting strap. Secure the switch and its coverplate, and test.

THE USES OF SCONCE LIGHTING

Wall sconces provide a splash of indirect light, creating the illusion that a room is larger than it is. For this reason, and because they are commonly placed slightly higher than eye level, keep the bulb wattage low.

In most cases wall sconces work best in conjunction with other lights rather than as the primary light source for a room. They work well for ambient light but are insufficient for specific tasks, such as reading. Install sconces 72 to 78 inches high. Any lower and you will bump into them; any higher and they will seem designed to light the ceiling rather than the room.

Typically it makes the most sense to add wall sconces to one wall requiring accent or indirect lighting. A few sconces go a long way, so keep them spaced more than 6 feet from each other.

ADDING UNDERCABINET LIGHTING

A kitchen is a brighter, more pleasant place to work when its countertops are illuminated by undercabinet fixtures. Undercabinet lighting provides a sparkling decorative effect and gives you excellent task lighting.

A 120-volt system requires hours of fishing and installing fixture boxes in one of the most crowded and complicated areas of the house. An attractive alternative is the low-voltage system shown here. Low-voltage halogen lights operated with a remote-controlled, surface-mounted switch can be installed in a day and look as good as a more permanent system.

YOU'LL NEED

TIME: About a day to install a switch and 10 lights.

SKILLS: Stripping and connecting wires, simple carpentry skills.

TOOLS: Screwdriver, drill, lineman's pliers, keyhole saw.

1 INSTALL THE LIGHTS AND TRANSFORMER.

Determine a location for each light fixture where it won't shine in your eyes as you work. Keep in mind halogen lights can be safely attached to wooden cabinets but get hot and should be kept away from plastic and paper goods. Remove the trim ring and lens from each fixture base and attach them with screws to the underside of the cabinets. (Be sure the screws are the right length so they do not poke up into your cabinet.) Align the fixtures so the bulbs face the same direction. Drill small holes to allow the wires to pass into your cabinet, and plug their ends into the power block located inside the cabinet. Coil excess wire inside the cabinet. Connect the power block to the transformer. Drill a hole and run a wire from the transformer to a 120-volt receptacle.

FLUORESCENT UNDERCABINET LIGHTING

Low-voltage halogen lighting is an easy improvement when cabinets are already installed. But if you are installing new cabinets, consider adding thin (1- to 1½-inch thick) fluorescent lights under the cabinets.

To install fluorescent lights, run standard electrical cable behind the walls. Run wires behind the cabinets, if possible, to avoid patching the walls. Or use raceway wiring attached to the underside of the cabinets (see pages 78–79).

2 ASSEMBLE THE LIGHTS.

Once the fixture bases are installed, snap the lens cover onto the reflector ring. Some undercabinet lighting kits come with a warning label to attach inside the cabinet door, cautioning users about the heat of the units.

3 INSTALL THE SWITCH.

The switch operates by battery power, so it can be installed anywhere in the kitchen and requires no wiring. Attach the switch housing by screwing it to the wall—use plastic anchors if you can't find a stud. Screw the coverplate to the switch housing.

Lighting positioned on the underside of kitchen wall cabinets provides bright illumination, but does not shine in the eyes of an adult standing at the counter.

You may choose to install low-voltage halogens (see page 71), but they get very hot. If you have only one or two lights to install, consider purchasing undercabinet fluorescent fixtures that plug into a nearby receptacle. If you want to add a section of lights controlled by one or two switches, you may choose to run cable and install a series of fluorescents.

Select fixtures that are 1½ inches thick. One-inch-thick fixtures are sleeker but more difficult to install because there is little room for cramming in wires.

This job is much easier to do while the wall cabinets are removed, so it is an ideal project when replacing wall cabinets. Mark the walls with lines that show precisely where the new cabinets will be installed, and run the wiring so that the cabinets will cover most (if not all) of the holes in the wall.

Local codes for under-cabinet lights vary; strict codes may require you to run conduit or armored cable, and you may be required to install an electrical box behind every fixture.

1 RUN THE CABLE.

See pages 140–147 for tips on running cable. This is much easier to do if the wall cabinets are not yet installed.

If you can, remove the countertop's backsplash and cut a channel that will later be covered when you replace the backsplash. Before you cut holes for the lights, check each light to determine where the cable will enter and exit. You may be able to cut holes small enough so they will be covered by the lights.

Drill holes in the studs, and install protective nailing plates. Run cable from a power source to the switch box. Then run cable from the switch box to the lights. Allow plenty of cable at each connection.

YOU'LL NEED

TIME: A day to run cable and install 6 or 7 lights.

SKILLS: Running cable, stripping and connecting wires, cutting and patching walls.

TOOLS: Drill, fish tape, lineman's pliers, pliers, stud finder, wire stripper, screwdriver, drywall saw.

RUNNING CONDUIT INSIDE A CABINET.

Rather than cutting holes in the wall, local codes may allow you to run conduit or armored cable inside the cabinets. Use elbow connections to direct the wires down into the light fixtures.

ADDING RACEWAY UNDER A CABINET.

Raceway wiring is another option; see pages 78–79 for installation tips. You will have to carefully cut several little pieces, but you'll save the trouble of cutting and patching walls.

② CLAMP THE CABLES.

Strip enough sheathing so the wires can reach
connections inside the light. Disassemble each light.
Clamp the cables to the light's housing as shown.

③ ATTACH THE LIGHTS.

Guide the cables into the wall as you push the housing
against the wall and the underside of the cabinet. Drive
screws to secure the housing.

④ WIRE THE LIGHTS.

Determine how long each wire needs
to be; plan splices in places where
there is ample room for the wire nuts.
Connect the ground wires (see page
139). Splice the white leads to the
white wires and the black leads to the
black wires. Snap the light together,
and add fluorescent tubes.

⑤ WIRE THE SWITCH.

Shut off the power. Install a remodel
box and run the cables through it.
Attach the cable at the power source.
Connect the ground wires (see page
139). Splice the two white wires
together, and connect the two black
wires to the switch. Restore power
and test the lights. Snap on the
light covers.

COVE LIGHTING.

A fluorescent fixture placed on top
of a wall cabinet throws dramatic
illumination upward and outward.
Because the fixture is not visible,
you can buy an inexpensive unit
and let the wiring hang out.

One of the easiest ways to upgrade your home's electrical system is to install special switches. Wiring them is rarely much more difficult than installing a standard switch.

There are many options, so choose the switch that best meets your needs. The least expensive dimmers have round switches that you twist. Sleeker options include the sliding dimmer shown, right, or dimmers that look like regular toggle switches. Other types allow you to choose a level of brightness and then turn the light on and off at that level. It turns on a light fixture whenever someone enters a room, staying on for a prescribed amount of time.

Some switches have limitations. An ordinary dimmer, for example, can only handle up to 600 watts, so it may not be able to operate a chandelier. For higher-wattage fixtures, buy special dimmers able to handle 800, 1,000, or 1,500 watts. (For more information on these and other switches, see pages 122–123.)

If you have ground wires, they all should be connected together in the box, no matter what kind of switch you are installing.

Always shut off the power before removing or installing a switch.

SINGLE-POLE DIMMER.

Most dimmers have wire leads instead of screw terminals. Hook up a single-pole dimmer as shown.

Most dimmers are larger than conventional switches, so you may have to rearrange wires in the box before you can fit one in. Don't force a dimmer in because the case might crack. If there are too many wires, order a thin-profile unit.

THREE-WAY DIMMER.

Three-way dimmers have three hot leads. Before you remove the old switch, determine which is the common terminal—it will be identified on the switch body or the screw will be darker-colored than the others. Hook the common wire to the new switch's common lead, and connect the other wires. (For more on three-way switches, see pages 89–91.)

SWITCH/RECEPTACLE.

In this wiring arrangement, the receptacle is always hot and not controlled by the switch. Connect the ground wires (see page 139). Attach a white pigtail to the silver terminal and splice it with the other white wires. Connect the feed wire to a terminal that has a connecting tab. Join the other black wire to the brass terminal that does not have a connecting tab.

PILOT-LIGHT SWITCH.

This switch has a bulb that glows when its fixture is on. Join the black feed wire to the brass terminal on the side that does not have a connecting tab. Pigtail two white wires and attach them to the silver terminal. Connect the black wire that leads to the fixture to the terminal on the side with the connecting tab.

YOU'LL NEED

TIME: About an hour to install most of the switches on these two pages.

SKILLS: Connecting wires.

TOOLS: Screwdriver, lineman's pliers, wire stripper.

MOTION-SENSOR SWITCH.

An infrared beam detects movement and turns on a light fixture. A time-delay feature lets you choose how long the light remains on. Connect the neutral wires to each other, not to the switch. Attach the black feed wire to one lead and connect the black wire that runs to the fixture to the other lead.

TIME-DELAY SWITCH.

You can program this switch to turn off a fixture with a delay ranging from 1 to 60 minutes. In addition to the clock timer switch shown, electronic switches with presettable delays are available. Connect the black leads to the black wires in the box, and join the white wires together, not to the switch.

FLUORESCENT DIMMER.

Fluorescent dimmer switches install the same way as incandescent dimmers (see page 74), but you must equip each lamp with a special ballast. Remove the fixture. Mark the wires with tape so you'll know where to refasten them. Remove the lamp holders and disconnect their wires by poking a nail or thin screwdriver into the terminals. Take off the old ballast and install a new dimming ballast. Reconnect the lamp holders. Reinstall the fluorescent fixture. If more than one fluorescent light is connected to a dimmer switch, all the bulbs must be the same size and share the same ballast (for replacing a ballast, see page 45).

DOUBLE SWITCH.

This unit has two switches that fit into a single-switch space. Attach the feed wire to a terminal on the side with the connecting tab. (This tab enables the wire to supply power to both switches.) Connect the two wires that lead to the two fixtures to the terminals on the other side, and join the white wires together, not to the switch.

PLUG-IN LAMP DIMMER.

A lamp dimmer is a simple way to provide variable-level lighting. To install it, just plug the dimmer cord into a receptacle and plug a lamp into the back of the dimmer plug. Turn the lamp switch on and control the lamp with the dimmer switch. You can place the dimmer near the lamp or in any convenient location you can reach with the cord.

MONEY SAVER

These switches give you greater control over your lighting and can save money as well: A dimmer switch enables you to operate a bulb at less than its full intensity so you save energy and prolong the life of the bulb. Time-delay and pilot-light switches are energy-efficient solutions too. You can also buy programmable switches to save money and provide security while you are on vacation. You can program them to turn lights on and off in a pattern that makes it appear you are still at home.

Fuses and circuit breakers protect the wiring in your home. A ground fault circuit interrupter (GFCI) protects people from getting a dangerous shock.

A GFCI has a microprocessor that senses tiny current leaks and shuts off the power instantly. In most circumstances a leak isn't a big problem. In properly grounded systems most of it is carried back to the service panel. What remains would scarcely give you a tickle. But if you are well grounded—standing on a wet lawn or touching a plumbing component, for example—that tiny bit of current would pass through your body on its way to the earth. As little as $\frac{1}{5}$ of an amp, just enough to light a 25-watt bulb, can be dangerous.

A GFCI connects to both wires of a circuit so it can continuously compare current levels flowing through the hot and neutral sides. These should always be equal. If the microprocessor senses a difference of just $\frac{1}{200}$ of an amp, it trips the circuit. Power is interrupted in $\frac{1}{40}$ of a second or less, cutting off the electricity before you're seriously hurt. Any ground fault is a potential hazard.

Plug-in GFCI

GFCI receptacle

GFCI breaker

GFCI OPTIONS.

There are three types of GFCIs: plug-ins, receptacles, and breakers. To install a portable plug-in unit, simply insert its blades into a receptacle and plug in the appliance. A GFCI receptacle replaces a conventional receptacle, and properly placed can protect other receptacles on the same circuit. Install a GFCI breaker into a service panel to protect a circuit.

If a tool or appliance is faulty, it can give you a serious shock even if its grounding wire is in good condition. So GFCI protection is a good idea anywhere you might be in contact with water while using electricity, such as in a kitchen, bathroom, or outdoors.

YOU'LL NEED

TIME: About 1 hour.

SKILLS: Connecting wires.

TOOLS: Screwdriver, lineman's pliers, wire stripper.

FOLLOW LOCAL CODES.

Electrical codes require GFCI receptacles in places where you're likely to ground an electrical appliance. In a kitchen codes often require GFCIs for all receptacles within 6 feet of a sink. All bathroom receptacles, as well as all outdoor receptacles, must be GFCI-protected.

WIRE A GFCI RECEPTACLE.

Attach a GFCI receptacle, above, connecting multiple wires with pigtails. Incoming power goes to the LINE terminals. LOAD lines carry power from the GFCI to other receptacles on the circuit. So if you install a GFCI as the first receptacle of a circuit, the entire circuit will be protected. If you are installing a GFCI at the end of a line, cap the load leads with wire connectors, or buy a version that protects only one receptacle.

SAFETY

A GFCI receptacle is bulkier than a standard receptacle, so it may be a tight fit in a box. If gently pushing the wires back doesn't help the GFCI fit, then don't force it. You might break the case or loosen the wire connections. Instead install a box extender.

Installing a GFCI breaker.

1 CONNECT HOT AND NEUTRAL WIRES.

You can clip a GFCI breaker into a service panel as you would an ordinary breaker (see page 115), but you must wire it differently. Shut off the main breaker and be careful not to touch the hot wires coming into the box. Select the circuit you wish to protect, unclip the old breaker from the hot bus bar, and slip it out of the service panel. Disconnect the hot wire from the old breaker and the neutral wire from the bus bar. Attach both wires to the setscrew terminals of the new GFCI breaker as shown. Strip ½ inch of insulation from the pigtail.

2 GROUND AND INSTALL THE BREAKER.

Loosen a terminal on the neutral bus bar, and connect the white pigtail by inserting the wire and tightening the screw. Clipping the GFCI breaker into place attaches it to the hot bus bar. Turn the power back on, set the breaker, and push the test button. The breaker should trip.

If you do not want to cut into your walls, fish wires, and patch and paint after adding a fixture, consider surface-mounted wiring. Surface-mounted components are available in metal or plastic and are comparatively easy to install. The system's main drawback is that it is fully visible. But for informal settings—a basement or a work room, for instance—it is a convenient alternative.

Shut off the power before connecting to existing receptacles.

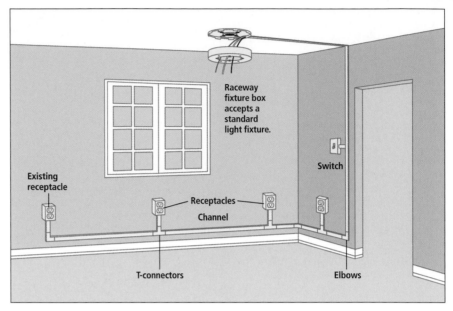

Raceway fixture box accepts a standard light fixture.

Switch

Existing receptacle

Receptacles

Channel

T-connectors

Elbows

BASEBOARD CHANNEL

A decorative and functional plastic baseboard channel can be added to an existing baseboard or even substituted for it. This type of channel is designed to simultaneously carry household wiring, coaxial cable, and telephone and computer lines. Extension boxes with receptacles, phone jacks, and coaxial hookups can be added along its length.

YOU'LL NEED

TIME: About 4 hours for a system like the one shown.

SKILLS: Connecting wires, measuring and cutting.

TOOLS: Hacksaw and miter box, tape measure, level, basic electrician's tools.

PLAN THE JOB.

Check your local codes. They probably limit surface, or raceway, wiring to dry locations where the walls are not subject to damage (as they are, for example, in a garage). Decide where you want the pieces to go, and measure carefully for all the runs. Take your calculations to your electrical supplier and have a salesperson help you choose the parts you need.

Starter-box extension frame

Source box

Existing receptacle

Plate

Channel

HOW THE PIECES GO TOGETHER.

A raceway system begins by tapping into an existing circuit at a receptacle. Select a receptacle on a circuit that has enough capacity for additional outlets (see pages 112–113). Install a starter box on the existing outlet so it can match up with the wall-mounted channel. Knockout holes allow you to extend the raceway channel from the starter box in any direction. Additional receptacles—as well as switches and light fixtures—mount directly on the wall or ceiling.

1 START AT THE BOX.

Shut off the power. Remove the receptacle and install the starter box. The receptacle will be reinstalled in the starter box later, as shown in Step 5. Map out the system from this starting point.

Wire holder clips

Baseboard

2 CUT AND ASSEMBLE COMPONENTS.

When you measure the channel sections for cutting, take into account the elbows, Ts, and other connectors. Cut the channels with a hacksaw and a miter box. Use extension connectors to tie the ends of the channels together and the Ts and elbows at the corners. Measure carefully from the floor, and use a level to make sure the receptacles are the same height.

3 ATTACH PARTS SECURELY.

Chances are the channels will be bumped by furniture and normal household traffic, so take care to attach them securely. Locate studs and drill screws into them where possible. Use plastic anchors in places you can't reach the studs.

Wire holder clips

4 RUN THE WIRES.

Run the wiring and hold it in place approximately every foot with specially designed clips. Be sure to leave 6 to 8 inches of wire at each outlet for room to strip and make the connections.

5 MAKE THE CONNECTIONS.

Attach all fixtures and receptacles (see pages 46–49). Connect to the existing receptacle, turn the power back on, and test the new fixtures and receptacles. Install the snap-on covers for the channels, fittings, and boxes.

A ceiling fan is heavy and vibrates continuously as it runs. So it must be firmly attached to the ceiling. The best approach is to install a fan-rated ceiling box designed to handle the extra load. Use a fan-rated box for any heavy ceiling fixture, such as a large chandelier.

The box may be either metal or a durable plastic. It should have deep, precisely machined screw holes to securely attach the mounting bolts.

CEILING FAN CLEARANCES AND CAPACITY

For safety–and to give the fan adequate space to effectively move air–use the clearances shown below. Select fan blades to suit the square footage of the room.

At least 10"

At least 18" to nearest wall

7' minimum to floor

Fan diameter (inches)	Room area (square feet)
36	96
42	144
48	288
52	400

YOU'LL NEED

TIME: Approximately 2 hours to remove an existing box and install a new one.

SKILLS: Basic carpentry skills, connecting cable.

TOOLS: Hammer, pry bar, keyhole or reciprocating saw, screwdriver, drill with screwdriver bit, wrench.

REMOVING A CEILING BOX.

Shut off the power. If the space above is an unfinished attic, disconnect the box from the attic. If you need to work from below, take care not to damage any wiring. You may need to enlarge the hole to get at the box. (You can install a medallion later to cover up the larger hole.) Use a reciprocating saw or a keyhole saw to cut through mounting nails.

INSTALLING A BRACKET INSTEAD OF A BOX.

In some cases you may choose to omit installing a fan-rated box, and instead firmly affix the ceiling fan's mounting plate directly to the ceiling. Drive two or three wood screws (not drywall screws, which are not strong enough) through the mounting plate and deep into a joist. Cover the ceiling box with a medallion.

REMOVING AN OLDER PANCAKE BOX.

An older box like this may be held in place with screws driven into lath or a joist and with a nut that attaches it to a center pipe. Once you pry out the box, you may need to cut the pipe as well; be careful not to damage the wires.

FAN BOX OPTIONS.

Some fan-rated boxes attach to the side of a joist. Others (as shown on the opposite page) attach between joists. Still others fit directly under the joist.

1 PUT THE BOX BRACE IN PLACE.

A braced box is usually the best choice. The box must be at least 1½ inches away from the side of a joist. If necessary enlarge the hole to accommodate the extra space. Thread the brace (with the box unattached) into the hole.

2 TIGHTEN THE BRACE.

Rotate the brace's shaft until it starts to tighten against the joists. Measure to make sure it is centered on the hole and is the correct height so the box will be flush with the ceiling. Firmly tighten the brace with a wrench.

3 ATTACH THE BOX.

Attach the U-bolt assembly onto the shaft; it should be centered on the hole. Clamp the cable to the box. Slide the box up over the bolts and tighten the nuts to hold it firmly.

INSTALLING FROM THE ATTIC.

If the space above is an unfinished attic, disconnect the old box from there. Add a new-work fan-rated box. Assemble the box onto the shaft, slide the box to the desired location, and fit the shaft between joists. Check to see if the bottom of the box is flush with the ceiling, then drive screws or nails to secure the brace.

INSTALLING A BOX BENEATH A JOIST.

If a joist is directly above the hole, running through the hole's center, install the box by driving two or three wood screws (not drywall screws) into the joist.

INSTALLING A CEILING FAN

Whether it's moving warm air downward for heat in the winter or circulating cool air in the summer, a ceiling fan can cut energy costs and help keep your home more comfortable all year.

Start with a strong, fan-rated box securely fastened to the ceiling (see pages 80–81). If you want to control the fan and the light separately, you can run three-wire cable from the fan to the switch box or install a remote-control fan.

Some fans come with lights. Others give you the option of having a fan only, or installing a light kit that you buy separately.

YOU'LL NEED

TIME: 3 or 4 hours to install a ceiling fan once the box is installed and wired.

SKILLS: Basic wiring skills.

TOOLS: Lineman's pliers, screwdriver, drill with screwdriver bit, wire stripper, tape measure.

1 ASSEMBLE THE FAN.

Follow the manufacturer's instructions for adding a downrod and installing the canopy. Take care to assemble the pieces in the correct order. Run the fan and light leads through the downrod.

2 ATTACH THE MOUNTING BRACKET.

Shut off the power. Anchor the mounting bracket firmly to the fan-rated box using the screws provided. Some models have rubber washers that sandwich between the bracket and the box to dampen sound and minimize vibration. Tug on the bracket to make sure it is strong.

Special switch

Remote-control transmitter

Receiver in fan

SWITCHING OPTIONS.

Most ceiling fans have two pull switches, one for the fan and one for the light. If you want to control the light and the fan separately from a wall switch, several options are available at a home center:

- Run three-wire cable from the fixture to the switch box and install a fan/light double switch (shown above left).
- Buy a fan that has a special wall switch that controls the fan and light separately through a standard two-wire cable (above).

- Install a remote-control switch (above). This is convenient but more expensive. You can control the fan and the light from anywhere in the room with a wireless transmitter. A receiver fits inside the fan's canopy. Some fans have built-in remote controls.

3 WIRE THE FIXTURE.

Most fans have a hook that allows you to hang it temporarily from the bracket while you work. Connect the ground lead (see page 139). If only two wires enter the box, splice the white lead to the white wire and splice both the black lead (for the fan) and the colored lead (for the light) to the black wire. If three wires enter the box, splice black to black and colored to colored.

4 ADD THE CANOPY.

It's important that the wires are neatly and securely tucked up and away in the box rather than hanging into the canopy; otherwise they could make noise when the fan runs. Slip the canopy onto the mounting bracket and tighten the screws to hold it firm.

5 ATTACH THE FAN BLADES.

Make sure the correct side of the fan blades face down, then screw a bracket onto each fan blade. Screw the brackets to the fan motor. After they are all installed, go back and tighten them.

6 WIRE THE LIGHT.

Remove the coverplate on the bottom of the fan to reveal the wiring for the fan. Find the white wire and the correct colored wire (see your manufacturer's instructions) and connect the leads for the light kit as directed. Tuck the wires back into the housing, push the light onto the housing, and secure with screws.

7 INSTALL THE SWITCH.

If the fan comes with a dedicated wall switch, install it according to the manufacturer's instructions. If you run three-wire cable from the fan for a double switch, connect the black lead from the fan to the fan switch and the red or colored lead to the light switch. Join the white wires together and splice any ground wires together in the box.

INSTALLING TELEPHONE AND TV WIRING

Telephone and cable (or satellite) TV companies will install extension wiring for you, but they may charge a hefty amount, even for running a simple surface-mounted extension line. Although it is not feasible for a homeowner to make extensive installations, it does make sense for you to run cable for extra telephones or a second TV. Before you add cable TV outlets, check with your cable TV provider to make sure you are allowed to add hardware and additional lines to the installation in your home.

You'll find that running wires for telephones and cable TV is easier than electrical wiring. There is no danger of shock and only one cable to run. Still, the same principles of installation and connection apply: Protect wire insulation from damage, and secure the connections.

The simplest way to install the cable is to tack or staple it to the wall. Although a common practice, this can be unsightly and a mess when you paint walls and molding. For a neater and more permanent installation, take the time to run the cable out of sight as shown on the opposite page.

as shown on the opposite page.

THE RIGHT CABLE

To avoid a noisy connection and possible damage to your phone system, use cable marked 22-AWC (often marked "line cord") or "category 5" to add a branch line. This solid-core cable is more expensive than stranded wires or filament wire, but well worth the investment. Stranded-wire extension cable, sold in 25- and 50-foot lengths, should only be used between the jack and the phone, not for adding new extensions.

Purchase shielded coaxial cable for television cables. It has a metal wrapping under the insulation. Nonshielded cable will probably cause interference and distortion.

YOU'LL NEED

TIME: Several hours for a typical extension of a television cable or telephone line.

SKILLS: Connecting wires, possibly some carpentry skills.

TOOLS: Drill, screwdriver, pliers, wire stripper, carpentry tools.

Telephone and cable jacks

Wireless Phone Jack System

Wall phone jack

In-wall phone jack

2-for-1 adapter jack

Surface-mounted jack

Modular phone plug

Coaxial jack

Combination phone and coaxial jack

Telephone cable

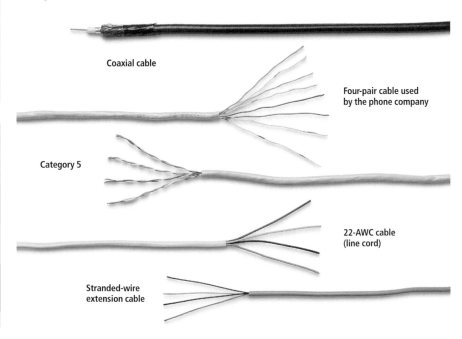

Coaxial cable

Four-pair cable used by the phone company

Category 5

22-AWC cable (line cord)

Stranded-wire extension cable

1   RUN A CABLE DOWN THE WALL.

Cut a hole in the wall where you want to locate an in-wall phone or cable jack. Attach a length of beaded chain to the end of the cable with electrician's tape. Drop the chain down through the hole. If you feel it hitting an obstruction, give it a wiggle.

2   GRAB THE CHAIN AT THE BOTTOM.

Once the chain drops far enough, drill a hole in the wall at the point where you want to retrieve the cable. (To hide the cable completely, remove the baseboard molding first.) Insert a bent piece of coat hanger wire, and root around until you hook the chain. Pull the chain through the hole until approximately 1 foot of cable sticks out.

3   INSTALL BOX AND JACK.

Determine where you want a new phone or coaxial cable jack, and cut out the wall as you would for an electrical box (see page 134). Pull about 8 inches of cable through the box. Install the box. For phone cable, strip the sheathing and insulation, and make connections as marked on the jack. At the phone junction box, connect the wires to the color-coded terminals.

4   HIDE CABLE UNDER CARPETING.

If you don't want to go to the trouble of pulling up your baseboard, it is often possible to hide most of the cable under wall-to-wall carpeting. Pry up only 2 feet of carpeting at a time, or you may have trouble getting it to reattach to the tack strip. Slip the cable underneath the carpet and push it firmly back in place as you go.

MAKE COAXIAL CONNECTIONS.

To make any type of coaxial connection, first attach male connectors to each cut cable end: Using strippers or a knife, strip ½ inch of outer sheathing; cut carefully so the underlying wire mesh stays intact. Fold back the wire mesh, and strip ⅜ inch of the plastic insulation. Slip on a crimp-type connector. The wire should run about 1/16 inch past the connector. Use a special coaxial crimping tool (above) to crimp the connection tight.

    Once the male connectors are attached, you can screw them onto a fitting, such as the splitter, above.

WIRING A CEILING FIXTURE

D epending on which way is easier to run cable, you can wire a ceiling fixture with the power coming into the box (as shown on this page) or with power coming into the switch (as shown on the opposite page).

Here, as with the configurations on the following six pages, the type of fixture doesn't matter. Whether it is a flush-mounted light, track lighting, a chandelier, or a ceiling fan, the rough wiring to the fixture is the same.

Power source

YOU'LL NEED

TIME: About 1 hour making connections, not including running the cable and installing boxes.

SKILLS: Basic electrical skills.

TOOLS: Lineman's pliers, needle-nose pliers, side-cutting pliers, wire stripper, cable ripper, screwdriver.

Power in

Junction box

Direction of power

Ground wire

Fixture box

Switch box

1 BEGIN MAKING CONNECTIONS.

Shut off the power. Install the fixture box and a switch box, and run cable as needed (see pages 132–135). Find a junction box or receptacle box (see page 93) that has power from a circuit you can use. Run two-wire cable from the junction box to the fixture box and from the fixture box to the switch. Connect the ground wires (see page 139). Attach all the black wires as shown. Note how the black wire picks up power at the junction box and carries it to the fixture box, then on to the switch.

Junction box

Black tape

Switch box

Fixture box

Black tape

2 COMPLETE THE CONNECTIONS.

Mark the white wire running from the switch box to the fixture box with black tape on both ends. Attach one end to the switch. At the fixture box, connect the black-taped white wire to the black fixture wire and the untaped white wire to the white fixture wire. At the junction box connect all white wires together. (For instructions to connect the wires, see pages 136–139.)

WIRING TWO CEILING FIXTURES

In this wiring configuration, power comes to the switch first, then goes to both of the fixtures. (A single light also can be wired this way.) A single switch can control many fixtures. Just extend the run from one to the next. If you have multiple fixtures on a single line, make sure the wattage or amperage total of the fixtures doesn't exceed the maximum indicated on the body of the switch.

Power source

YOU'LL NEED

TIME: About 1½ hours to plan and complete the connections, not including running the cable and installing boxes.

SKILLS: Basic electrical skills.

TOOLS: Lineman's pliers, needle-nose pliers, side-cutting pliers, wire stripper, cable ripper, screwdriver.

2-wire cable · Second fixture box · Direction of power · First fixture box · 2-wire cable · Switch box · 2-wire cable · Power in

1 BEGIN MAKING CONNECTIONS.

Shut off the power. Install the fixture boxes and a switch box, and run cable as needed (see pages 132–147). Find a junction box or receptacle box (see page 93) that has power from a circuit you can use. Run two-wire cable from the junction box to the switch box (see pages 140–147 for instructions on running cable). Then run the cable from the switch box to the first fixture box, and from that box to the next fixture box. Connect the ground wires (see page 139). At the switch box hook both black wires to the terminals. The current in the black wire passes through the switch to the first fixture box.

Second fixture box · First fixture box · Switch box

2 COMPLETE THE CONNECTIONS.

At the switch box connect the two white wires together. At the first fixture box, join all three black wires together and connect all three white wires together. At the second fixture box, attach the black wires together and connect the white wires together. Note that you also can control two or more fixtures with the power coming to the fixture, but it's more complicated. Route the power as on the facing page, and attach the second fixture's black wire to the black-taped white wire in the first fixture box. (For instructions to connect the wires, see pages 136–139.)

WIRING SEPARATE SWITCHES

If you are installing ceiling fixtures and a switch box, with a little more work you can provide individual switches for the fixtures. Use a two-gang box for the switches or a double switch in a single box, and run three-wire cable between the fixtures and to the switch. Power comes to the fixtures through two-wire cable. Electricians like three-wire cable because in many instances it allows the use of one cable instead of two.

To junction box

Power in

2-wire cable to junction box

3-wire cable

First fixture box

3-wire cable

Direction of power

Switch box

Second fixture box

Pigtail   Pigtail

1 BEGIN MAKING CONNECTIONS.

Shut off the power. Install the fixture boxes and a switch box, and run cable as needed (see pages 132–147). Run two-wire cable from a junction box to the first fixture box. Run three-wire cable from the first to the second fixture box, and from there to the switch box. Connect all ground wires (see page 139). Bring power to the switches by attaching the black wires in all three boxes as shown. In the switch box cut pigtails (short pieces of wire) and connect them to the switches.

2-wire cable   3-wire cable   3-wire cable

First fixture box

Second fixture box

Black tape

Switch box

Black tape

2 COMPLETE THE CONNECTIONS.

At the switch box connect the red wire to a switch and the white wire to the other switch. Wrap black tape on the white wire, both at the switch box and at the fixture box to show that it is hot. At the second fixture box, join the two red wires together. At both fixture boxes connect the hot and neutral wires to the fixture wires as shown. Or install this wiring configuration with power coming to the switch. Split the incoming black wire, and run the outgoing red and black wires to the fixtures. The neutral white wire, shared by both switches, passes on through.

WIRING THREE-WAY SWITCHES

Three-way switches control power to a fixture from two separate points, allowing you to control a ceiling light from either side of a room. Three-way switches use a three-wire system that has a power wire and two interconnecting wires called travelers. Unless you have metal conduit or armored cable, you also need a fourth, grounding wire. Power comes in through one switch, then travels to the fixture and to the second switch (see page 27 for more about three-way switches).

Power source

3-wire cable · 3-wire cable · First switch box · Traveler wires · Fixture box · Direction of power · Black tape · Common terminal · Black tape · Second switch box · Common terminal · Power in · 2-wire cable · Traveler wires

① BEGIN MAKING CONNECTIONS.

Shut off the power. Install the switch boxes and a fixture box, and run cable as needed (see pages 132–147). Run two-wire cable from a junction box or a receptacle box (see page 93) to the first switch box. Run three-wire cable from the first switch box to the fixture box, and from the fixture box to the second switch box. Connect all ground wires (see page 139). At the first switch box, connect the hot wire to the common terminal on the switch (it is either labeled or darker than the other two). Attach traveler wires to the other two terminals. At the second switch box, attach the red and white wires to the noncommon terminals of the switch. Wrap a piece of black tape on the white wire, both here and at the fixture box. At the fixture box connect the two red wires, and join the marked white wire to the black wire that comes from the first switch.

3-wire cable · 3-wire cable · First switch box · Second switch box · 2-wire cable

② COMPLETE THE CONNECTIONS.

At the second switch box, connect the black wire to the common terminal on the switch. This completes the hot portion of the circuit. At the first switch box, attach the two white wires. At the fixture box connect the white and black wires to the fixture. Once completed, either switch will operate the light.

Page 89 shows how to wire three-way switches when the light is between two switches. This page shows the light beyond both switches, and includes an example with a three-way dimmer. (Only one of the two switches can be a dimmer.)

For this configuration run three-wire cable between the switches. Power comes into the first switch and out of the second on just two wires.

Power source

Power in

2-wire cable

First switch box

Ground wire

Common terminal

Fixture box

2-wire cable

Second switch box

Ground wire

Traveler wires

3-wire cable

3-way dimmer

1 BEGIN MAKING CONNECTIONS.

Shut off the power. Install the switch boxes and a fixture box, and run cable as needed (see pages 132–147). Run two-wire cable from a junction box or a receptacle box (see page 93) to the first switch box. Run three-wire cable from the first switch box to the second, and two-wire cable from the second switch box to the fixture box. Connect the ground wires (see page 139). At the first switch box, attach the black (hot) wire of the power source to the switch's common terminal. Connect traveler wires to the other terminals. At the second switch box, connect the travelers. (Note: A three-way dimmer can burn out if hooked up incorrectly. Check it by setting up the circuit with ordinary three-way switches and turning on the power. Then replace one switch with a dimmer.)

2-wire cable

First switch box

Fixture box

2-wire cable

Second switch box

2-wire cable

2 COMPLETE THE CONNECTIONS.

At the second switch box, connect the black wire that goes to the fixture box with the dimmer's common wire. Join the two white wires. At the first switch box, attach the white wires. At the fixture box connect black to black wires and white to white wires. Install the switches, switchplates, and the light fixture.

WIRING THREE-WAYS, POWER TO FIXTURE

In this situation power comes to the light fixture, then proceeds to the two switches. A two-wire cable runs to the fixture and to the the first switch box. A three-wire cable runs only from switch box to switch box.

Power source

YOU'LL NEED

TIME: 1½ hours after running cable and installing boxes.

SKILLS: Basic electrical skills.

TOOLS: See opposite page.

ABC'S OF THREE-WAYS

Follow these principles when wiring three-way switches:
A. Always attach the incoming hot (black) wire to the common terminal of the first switch.
B. Use traveler wires to connect the traveler terminals on the switches to each other, never to the light.
C. Connect the common terminal of the second switch to the black wire from the fixture.

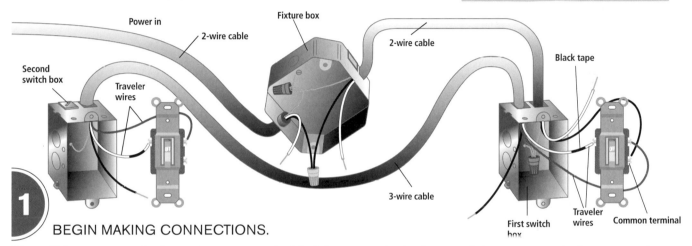

Power in
2-wire cable
Fixture box
2-wire cable
Black tape
Second switch box
Traveler wires
3-wire cable
First switch box
Traveler wires
Common terminal

1 BEGIN MAKING CONNECTIONS.

Shut off the power. At the fixture box connect the black hot wires. At the first switch box, connect the hot wire to the common terminal and the traveler wires to the other terminals. Wrap a piece of black tape on either end of the white wire to show that it is hot. At the second switch box, attach the traveler wires.

2-wire cable
Fixture box
2-wire cable
3-wire cable
First switch box
Second switch box
Common terminal

2 COMPLETE THE CONNECTIONS.

At the second switch box, connect the switch's common wire to the black wire leading to the fixture box. Attach the two white wires. At the first switch box, connect the white wires. At the fixture box connect black to black wires and white to white wires. Install the switches, switchplates, and the light fixture.

WIRING FOUR-WAY SWITCHES

To control a fixture from three or more different switches, use one or more four-way switches. You can install any number of them between a pair of three-way switches. In four-way situations the first and last switches must always be three-ways.

Here incoming power flows from switch to switch to switch then to the fixture, but it also could take one of the routes previously illustrated.

Power source

YOU'LL NEED

TIME: About 2 hours to make the connections for a fixture and three switches, not including running the cable and installing boxes.

SKILLS: Basic electrical skills.

TOOLS: Lineman's pliers, needle-nose pliers, side-cutting pliers, wire stripper, cable ripper, screwdriver.

1 BEGIN MAKING CONNECTIONS.

Shut off the power. Install the switch boxes and a fixture box, and run cable as needed (see pages 132–147). Run two-wire cable from a junction box or a receptacle box (see page 93) to the first switch box. Run three-wire cable from the first switch box to the second and third, and two-wire cable from the third switch box to the fixture box. Connect all ground wires. At the first switch box, attach the black wire from the power source to the switch's common terminal. Connect the traveler wires to the other terminals. At the second and third switches, connect the traveler wires as shown. The four-way switch carries only traveler wires.

2 COMPLETE THE CONNECTIONS.

At the third switch connect the fixture box's black wire to the common terminal. Join the white wires together. Attach the white wires at the first and second switch boxes. Connect the fixture to the two wires at the fixture box and install the switches and switchplates. Once completed you can turn the fixture on and off from any of the three switches.

ADDING RECEPTACLES

O nce you find a usable power source, adding a receptacle is easy to figure out. Most of the work involves cutting the wall, installing a box, fishing the cable, and patching the wall.

Here you can tap into a receptacle at the end of the run. If the receptacle is in the middle of the run, it will have wires running to all of its terminals. Use wire nuts to connect a new line; see page 28.

YOU'LL NEED

TIME: About 1 hour to make connections, not including running the cable and installing boxes.

SKILLS: Basic electrical skills.

TOOLS: Lineman's pliers, needle-nose pliers, side-cutting pliers, wire stripper, cable ripper, screwdriver.

1 BEGIN MAKING CONNECTIONS.

Shut off the power. Find a receptacle box where you can draw power without overcrowding the box or overloading the circuit. (You also can draw power from a junction box. Just connect the hot and neutral wires to the receptacle.) Install the new receptacle box. Run a two-wire cable from the existing box to the new box. Remove the screws that secure the existing receptacle to the box, and pull it out so you can work on it. Connect the ground wires in both boxes as shown.

2 COMPLETE THE CONNECTIONS.

At the existing box connect the black wire to the hot receptacle terminal, which is brass-colored. Attach the white wire to the other terminal. At the new box, also connect the black wire to the hot terminal and the white wire to the other terminal. Wrap both receptacles with electrician's tape so all the terminals are covered. Fasten both receptacles in place, turn on the power, and test your installation. Finally attach the receptacle plates.

ADDING 240-VOLT RECEPTACLES

Some 240-volt equipment—central air-conditioning units and electric water heaters, for example—have no plugs and are wired directly into junction boxes because they do not need to be moved. Ranges, clothes dryers, and other appliances have cords and plugs and require special receptacles.

The wiring requirements for 240-volt circuits are specific. For a 30-amp dryer, use a 30-amp breaker and 10-gauge wire. For a 50-amp range, use a 50-amp breaker and 6-gauge wire. Choose a receptacle designed to provide the correct amperage for your appliance and with holes to match the prongs on the plug.

►CAUTION

DANGER! HIGH VOLTAGE!

Wiring for 240-volt receptacles is no different from regular 120 lines, except that the danger is much, much greater. Even if you are dry and wearing rubber-soled shoes, a jolt of this current could seriously harm or even kill you. Check and double-check that the power is off before installing a 240-volt receptacle. This is one job where you may want to call in an experienced electrician, just for safety's sake.

YOU'LL NEED

TIME: About 1 hour to install a 240-volt receptacle after the wiring is completed.

SKILLS: Running cable, stripping and connecting wires.

TOOLS: Screwdriver, wire stripper, lineman's pliers.

240-VOLT WIRING.

Shut off the power. Wiring starts at a 240-volt breaker or fuse at the service panel and ends at a specially designed receptacle. A 240-volt circuit should supply only one appliance; no other receptacles can be attached to it. Connect 120-volt wires to a breaker and the neutral wire to the neutral bus bar (see pages 114–115).

DRYER RECEPTACLE.

Install a box and run 10/3 cable or four 10-gauge wires through conduit from a 30-amp, 240-volt double breaker in the service panel to the box. Connect the ground wire (see page 139). Strip and connect the other three wires to the terminals.

FLOOR-MOUNTED 240-VOLT RECEPTACLE.

If no outlet box is available, you can install this unit on the floor. Position it so it won't get bumped when you move the appliance. Remove the cover and connect the neutral wire to the terminal marked "white" and the red and black wires to the other terminals. The neutral wire serves as the ground for this receptacle.

AIR-CONDITIONER RECEPTACLE.

Many large air-conditioners plug into a 20-amp, 240-volt receptacle. Install a box and run 12/2 cable or three 12-gauge wires from a 20-amp, 240-volt double breaker in the service panel to the box. Connect the ground wire (see page 139). Mark the white wire black. Strip the wires and connect them to the terminals.

Examine a standard duplex receptacle and you'll see that each set of terminals on either side connects to a small metal tab—one silver-colored, one brass-colored. If you break this bridge, the upper and lower receptacles can be used independently, one controlled by a switch and one functioning like a standard receptacle. A split receptacle is handy when you want to turn a living room lamp on and off from a wall switch, for example, but still want to leave half of the receptacle for general use. Sometimes you may need a split receptacle when you want to supply the two outlets of a heavily used receptacle with two different circuits.

YOU'LL NEED

TIME: About 1 hour to make the connections, with the cables and boxes in place.

SKILLS: Basic electrical skills.

TOOLS: Screwdriver, wire stripper, lineman's pliers, needle-nose pliers.

Outlet box

Switch box

1 INSTALL CABLE AND BOXES.

Shut off the power. Disconnect the receptacle and run two-wire cable to a switch box. Hook up the ground wires.

Pigtail

2 ATTACH AND CONNECT BLACK WIRES.

Route power to the switch by tying the two black wires together with a pigtail at the receptacle box. Connect the black wire to the switch.

Black tape indicates wire is hot.

Switch box

3 CONTINUE WIRING AND SPLIT OUTLETS.

Add black tape to both ends of the white wire that runs between the boxes to show that it's hot. Connect it to the switch and receptacle terminals. Attach the remaining black wire to the receptacle. Snap off the brass tab with needle-nose pliers to split the outlets. Leave the silver-colored metal tab in place.

Outlet box

Switched receptacle

To switch

4 COMPLETE THE WIRING.

Connect the white and ground wires to the receptacle, screw the receptacle and switch to their boxes, turn on the power, and test. In this example the upper outlet will be live only when the switch is on. The lower one remains on at all times.

ADDING LOW-VOLTAGE OUTDOOR WIRING

These lights are inexpensive and very easy to install. They are not as bright as standard-voltage lights, but they provide enough illumination to light a path or showcase landscaping.

Plan the route of your lights, and decide how many you need. Then purchase a kit that contains the lights, the cable, and a transformer.

You will need to plug the transformer into a GFCI-protected receptacle. If you need a new outdoor receptacle, see page 98.

LIGHT OPTIONS.

You will find a wide selection of low-voltage lights for outdoor use at your local home center. Path lights direct illumination downward. Well lights barely protrude out of the ground, directing light upward.

YOU'LL NEED

TIME: Several hours to install a transformer and 10 to 15 lights.

SKILLS: No special skills required.

TOOLS: Screwdriver, drill with screwdriver bit, shovel.

1 PLACE THE LIGHTS.

Determine your layout, and arrange the lights where they will go. To insert a light into the ground, first try poking it in. If the ground is hard, slice it with a shovel, and poke the light into the slice.

2 RUN THE CABLE.

Route the cable from the transformer's location to the lights.

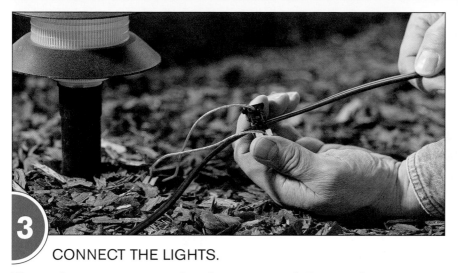

3 CONNECT THE LIGHTS.

Electrical connections are quick and require no tools. Position the two parts of a light's connector over the cable, then snap them together on the cable.

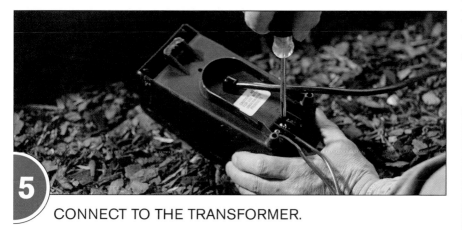

5 CONNECT TO THE TRANSFORMER.

Strip the wire ends and connect them to the transformer's terminals.

6 INSTALL THE TRANSFORMER.

Fasten the transformer to the house in a location where it is unlikely to be bumped. Plug into a GFCI receptacle with an in-use watertight cover.

7 PROGRAM THE TRANSFORMER.

The transformer can be set to turn lights on when it gets dark, or you may choose to program a timer.

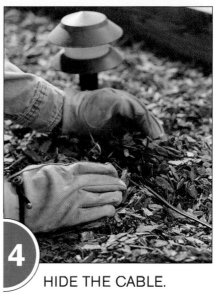

4 HIDE THE CABLE.

Because it carries only 12 volts, the wiring is not dangerous. Dig a shallow trench, lay the cable in the trench, and cover it with soil, sod, or mulch.

SOLAR LIGHT.

The easiest way to install a light fixture is to poke a solar light into the ground. It will absorb and store electricity during the day, and shine at night.

The easiest way to bring power to the outside of your house is to install a receptacle directly behind an existing interior receptacle. If you need to place the outdoor receptacle elsewhere, see pages 140–146 for ideas on fishing the cable. Be sure that the interior receptacle box you choose has room for new wires. Check to make sure you will not overload the circuit (see pages 112–113). Codes usually require a GFCI receptacle with a weatherproof coverplate and a spring-loaded door.

YOU'LL NEED

TIME: Approximately 3 hours, barring unexpected obstacles.

SKILLS: Basic electrical skills.

TOOLS: Drill with spade bit and perhaps a bit extension, screwdriver, lineman's pliers; a jigsaw, saber saw, or keyhole saw. If you have a masonry exterior, a masonry bit, cold chisel, and hammer.

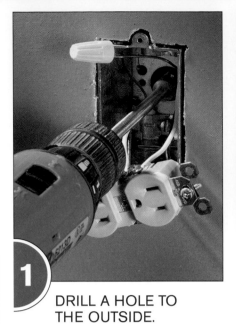

1 DRILL A HOLE TO THE OUTSIDE.

Shut off the power. Remove the faceplate and the interior outlet. To accurately locate your new receptacle, create a knockout hole in the back of the box, and drill a hole through the house to the outside. To make sure you have room for a box on each side (the wall may not be thick enough), drill off to the side.

2 CUT THE EXTERIOR OPENING.

Find the hole on the outside of your house, and draw an outline of the new box (see page 134). Drill a hole at each corner of the box, and cut with a jigsaw. If you have a masonry exterior, drill a series of closely spaced holes with a masonry bit. Knock out the hole with a cold chisel and hammer.

3 CONNECT THE CABLE.

Cut a piece of cable long enough to allow you working room. Connect it to the interior box—you will need a helper to reach through the exterior hole and hold the locknut in position while you tighten the locknut. Attach the cable to the exterior box too.

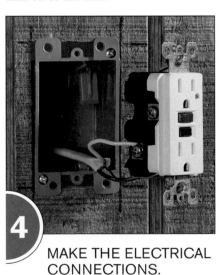

4 MAKE THE ELECTRICAL CONNECTIONS.

With the box pushed into place, strip the sheathing and the ends of the wires, and make connections on both ends of the cable (see pages 138–139). Be sure to connect to the "line" terminals on the GFCI receptacle and the load terminals on the existing interior receptacle.

5 INSTALL THE BOX AND COVER.

Attach the box firmly in place. With a masonry wall insert screws into the back of the box and attach them to a framing member, or mortar the box in place. Fasten the GFCI receptacle to the box. Finally add the gasket and weatherproof coverplate.

INSTALLING OUTDOOR LIGHTING

If you have eaves overhanging an exterior door, it makes sense to install a light there, where it will be better protected from weather than a wall-mounted unit would be. You're also likely to find it easy to run cable from an attic junction box to the eaves.

Consider installing a motion-detector floodlight. These are quite inexpensive, and if you wire it to be controlled with a regular wall switch, you can turn off the motion-sensing feature.

YOU'LL NEED

TIME: Approximately 4 hours, barring unexpected obstacles.

SKILLS: Basic electrical skills, measuring and cutting eaves.

TOOLS: Screwdriver, lineman's pliers, drill, saber saw or keyhole saw, fish tape.

1 CUT A HOLE IN THE EAVES.

Shut off the power. Draw an outline of the new box. (A retrofit box with wings for attaching to the eaves will probably work best.) Drill starter holes, then cut the hole with a saber saw or a keyhole saw.

2 RUN THE CABLE, INSTALL THE BOX.

Fish cable and make connections to an interior switch (see pages 134–147). Connect the cable to the new box, and firmly attach the box to the eaves.

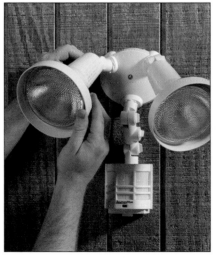

3 WIRE THE FLOODLIGHT.

Connect the wires to the floodlight using wire connectors, and screw the light firmly to the box. If your unit has a motion detector, wait until nighttime and adjust it so it turns on as people approach the door.

CAREFULLY ADJUST MOTION SENSOR

Adjusting a motion-sensor light is best done at night. Aim the light so it helps you but doesn't bother neighbors or passersby. Then set the light-on time; many lights offer 2, 5, or 10 minutes.

Point the motion sensor toward the protected area and set the range control to the middle position. Walk toward the light to see when it turns on. At the same time make sure it does not come on when you don't want it to—for instance, when you walk by on the sidewalk. Aim the motion sensor or adjust the range control to get it right.

ADDING A BATHROOM VENT FAN/LIGHT

A vent fan removes moisture and odor from a bathroom. Most models come with a light as well, and some also include a night-light or a heat lamp. A unit with a heat lamp may require a separate circuit because it uses much more amperage.

You can put the fan and the light on separate switches, but some codes require the fan to switch on with the light.

YOU'LL NEED

TIME: About a day to install a fan and run ductwork.

SKILLS: Basic electrical skills, carpentry skills.

TOOLS: Screwdriver, drill, lineman's pliers, wire stripper, drywall saw or jigsaw.

IDENTIFY VENTING OPTIONS.

Plan the route of the vent before you start installation. The shorter and straighter the duct run, the better the fan will suck air out of the bathroom and send it outside. A wall or eave vent, such as the one pictured here, is easiest to install. If necessary you can install a vent on the roof. Avoid cutting joists, wall studs, or roof-truss members so you won't weaken your framing.

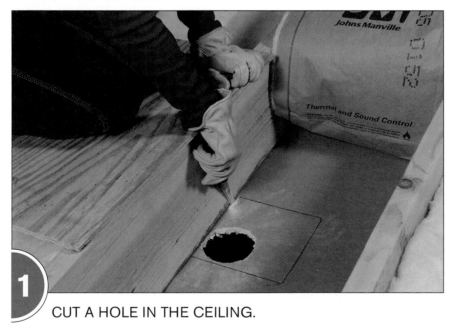

1 CUT A HOLE IN THE CEILING.

Shut off the power. If you have an existing light fixture, remove the ceiling box (see page 62). Use the fan's housing as a template to mark for the hole, next to a joist. Cut the hole (either from above or below) using a drywall saw or jigsaw.

2 ATTACH THE FAN BODY.

Disassemble the fan. If the fan requires three-wire cable, run it from the switch box to the fan. If insulation is present, cut pieces of lumber to fit between the joists and install them to keep the insulation several inches away from the fan. Hold the fan so its bottom edge is flush with the ceiling and fasten it to the joists with screws or nails.

3 INSTALL A VENT CAP.

Use a long bit to drill a locator hole from inside the attic. From the outside cut a hole for the vent cap using a jigsaw or reciprocating saw. Attach a length of duct to the vent cap, fastening it with screws and professional-quality duct tape. Run a bead of caulk around the hole, and slide the vent cap to the wall. Attach it with screws or nails.

4 RUN THE DUCTWORK.

Run solid or flexible ducting from the vent cap to the fan. If possible use a short, straight piece. If you use flexible ducting, cut it precisely to length rather than allowing it to loop around or bunch up. Fasten the joints with clamps, then wrap with duct tape.

5 WIRE THE FAN.

Reassemble the fan. Strip the sheathing and the wire ends, and clamp the cable to the fan housing (see pages 136–37). Connect the wiring according to manufacturer's directions. Connect the grounds (see page 139) and splice the white wires together. For a fan/light that is controlled by separate switches, connect the fan's lead to the black wire and the light's lead to the red wire.

6 WIRE THE SWITCH.

See page 27 for basic ways to wire a switch. If power enters the switch box and separate switches will control the light and the fan, connect the grounds and splice the white wires. Put two pigtails on the feeder wire and connect them to the brass terminals. Attach the red wire to one silver terminal and the black wire to the other silver terminal.

TIMER SWITCH FOR A FAN.

To ensure that a fan or heater is not left on all day, you can install a timer switch for the fan or heater and a standard switch for the light. You will need a double-gang box.

INSTALLING AN ATTIC FAN

On a hot summer day, the temperature in an attic can reach 150 degrees Fahrenheit or more. Turbine-type roof ventilators can help, but because they depend on wind to supplement the upward draft of hot air, you're out of luck on a still day when the heat buildup may be most intense.

A thermostat-controlled attic fan, mounted in the roof or a gable-end wall, automatically turns the fan on to vent overheated attics.

HOW BIG A FAN DO YOU NEED?

To determine how powerful a unit to buy, multiply the square footage of your attic by 0.7. Add 15 percent if your roofing is dark-colored—it will absorb more heat from sunlight than a lighter, more reflective roofing color. The resulting number tells you the cubic feet per minute (CFM) that your fan should pull.

YOU'LL NEED

TIME: A full day, with a helper.

SKILLS: Basic electrical and carpentry skills.

TOOLS: Ladder to get to the roof, roof jacks to provide a safe standing place if the roof is steep, drill, jigsaw or reciprocating saw, utility knife, hammer, screwdriver, lineman's pliers.

1 DRILL A LOCATING HOLE.

Position your fan as close to the ridge as you can to minimize the amount of hot air that will build up in the attic area above the fan. Choose a slope of the roof that's not visible from the street. Go into the attic and pick a pair of rafters close to the attic's center. Measure to a point midway between them. Drill up through the roof at this point. Leave the drill bit in place or push a piece of wire up through the hole as a marker.

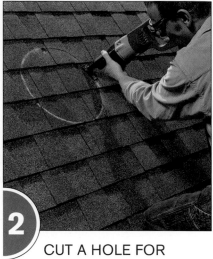

2 CUT A HOLE FOR THE FAN.

The manufacturer will provide a template or exact dimensions for the hole. You may adjust the position of the hole up or down a few inches in order to minimize the number of shingles you need to cut. Cut through the roofing and the sheathing using a reciprocating saw or a heavy-duty jigsaw. You may need to trim back some shingles as well.

COMBINE WHOLE-HOUSE FANS AND ATTIC FANS

Depending on your climate and use pattern, it may make economic sense to combine a thermostat-controlled fan with a whole-house fan. Here's why:

Even after sundown super-heated air continues to put a heavy strain on your home's air-conditioning system. By improving attic ventilation you can cut cooling costs as much as 30 percent.

A whole-house fan will pull a strong, steady draft up through the house—and push air out of the attic—on those days when you choose not to use the air-conditioning. It is not, however, effective to use a whole-house fan while the air-conditioning is on.

GABLE FAN.

You may choose to install a gable fan rather than a roof-mounted fan, especially if you already have a louvered cutout in the gable. It's easier to install because you don't have to cut a hole in the roof. Position it as high as possible, and wire it as you would a roof fan.

3 INSTALL THE FAN.

Pry up under shingles to loosen and remove roofing nails so you can slip the fan's flange all the way in. Slide the fan into position, centered over the hole.

4 ATTACH AND WEATHER-PROOF THE FAN.

The upper two-thirds of the fan's flange should be covered with shingles; the lower one-third should rest on top of the shingles. Drive roofing nails as recommended by the manufacturer, and coat any exposed nails with roofing cement.

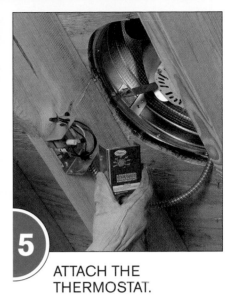

5 ATTACH THE THERMOSTAT.

Back in the attic, screw the thermostat switch to a stud or rafter above the fan and out of the air stream it will create. Remove the box coverplate.

6 MAKE THE WIRING CONNECTIONS.

Run cable from a junction box to the thermostat. Install cable to an accessible switch that can be used to override the automatic control. Follow the fan manufacturer's instructions for wiring. If directions weren't provided make the connections as indicated above, using wire connectors.

7 TEST AND ADJUST.

Turn on the power, and test your installation. An adjusting screw in the thermostat box lets you set the temperature that will activate the fan. The temperature setting will vary depending on your roof and the fan's capacity. Consult the manufacturer's instructions for the right temperature for your attic.

BUILDING A DEFENSE AGAINST HUMIDITY

If your area has high humidity, consider an attic fan with both a humidistat and thermostat. A humidistat senses humidity in the same way a thermostat reads the temperature, giving you another measurement for controlling the comfort level of your home.

On humid days an attic fan can make your home more comfortable by removing some of the moist air. Keeping attic moisture under control also helps prevent your fiberglass insulation from compacting and losing its effectiveness.

INSTALLING A WHOLE-HOUSE FAN

Before you select a whole-house fan, plan the overall venting of your house. The fan should pull air through open windows and doors on the lower floors and out through vents in the attic, eaves, and gables. Without adequate openings below and above the fan, it will not be able to do its job. Leave at least 2 feet of clearance between the fan and any obstructions. If you stack your attic with boxes, the fan may not have room to breathe, which will make it noisy as well as inefficient. Installation is not as difficult as you may think: The fan sits on top of the joists in the attic, so cutting and reframing aren't necessary.

CHOOSING A FAN

Buy a fan that's rated to pull a minimum cubic feet per minute (CFM) equal to the square footage of your house multiplied by three.

Will you really vent the whole house? If you plan to open the windows of just a few rooms, use only their square footage to figure the needed CFM.

Often a hall is the best spot for a fan. Will it fit yours? Fans designed to vent houses larger than 1,800 square feet (5,400 CFM) generally have louver panels of 38 inches or more—too wide for some hallways.

YOU'LL NEED

TIME: About a day, if fishing the cable is straightforward.

SKILLS: Basic electrical and carpentry skills.

TOOLS: Drill, saber saw, screwdriver, lineman's pliers, drywall saw, wire stripper.

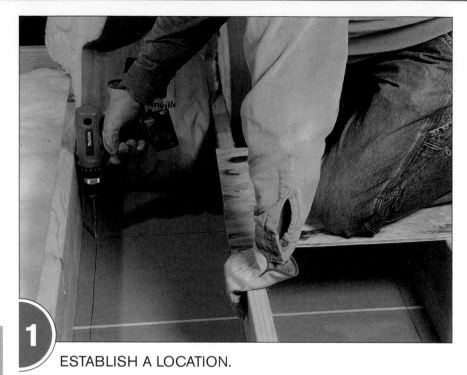

① ESTABLISH A LOCATION.

Find a spot for the fan—the top-floor hallway ceiling is the usual place. Measure from a point common to the hall and the attic, choose a location for the fan, and clear away the insulation. Beside the joists drill locator holes for cutting away the drywall or plaster. Cut a hole in the ceiling from below. Don't cut any joists.

② INSTALL THE FAN.

Remove any insulation that is in the way. You may need to install pieces of blocking to fill the spaces between the joists; or install plastic baffles supplied with the fan. (There should be no open space on the sides.) Build a frame of flat-laid 2×4s on top of the joists. Set the fan on top. Fasten it firmly with screws so it will not vibrate.

③ WIRE A JUNCTION BOX.

The fan likely comes with a short length of armored cable. If a junction box is not close enough for the cable to reach, install one. Bring power to the box via two-wire cable; make sure the fan will not overload the circuit (see pages 112–13). Clamp the fan's cable to the box, and also run three-wire cable to a switch box located in the room below.

Mark as black the white wire from the switch. Connect the grounds, and splice all the unmarked white wires. Splice the marked white wire with the black wire that goes to the fan. Splice the other black wires, as well as the red wires.

⑤ INSTALL THE COVER.

From below position the louver panel up against the ceiling so it covers the hole. Attach it to the ceiling by driving screws up into the joists. Test the louvers to make sure they open and close freely.

④ WIRE THE SWITCH.

Shut off the power. Clamp cable to a remodel box and install it in the switch hole. To install a two-level switch like this, connect the grounds. Mark the white wire black and splice it to the black switch lead. Splice the red wire to the red lead and the black wire to the blue lead.

ANOTHER WIRING ARRANGEMENT.

Shut off the power. If no power is available in the attic, you can bring power to the switch box first. At the switch box connect the grounds, splice the white wires, and connect the black wires to the switch's leads or terminals. In the junction box attach the grounds, splice the white wires, and splice the black wires.

INSTALLING A RANGE HOOD

A typical range hood has a light and also a fan that sucks odors out of the kitchen. The fan and the light are controlled by a switch on the fan, so it is not necessary to install a wall switch.

The bottom of the range hood should be about 24 inches above the range, or 60 inches above the floor. Usually it is attached to the underside of a wall cabinet that is 30 inches above the range.

YOU'LL NEED

TIME: Most of a day to run ducting outside, run cable, and install the range hood.

SKILLS: Basic carpentry skills, basic electrical skills.

TOOLS: Drill, drywall saw, jigsaw or reciprocating saw, screwdriver, lineman's pliers, wire stripper, tin snips.

1 MARK FOR THE HOLES.

Disassemble the fan, and use a hammer and pliers to remove the knockouts for the vent and the cable.

Hold the fan housing in place and trace the locations of the two holes.

2 CUT THE HOLES.

Cut the drywall or plaster with a drywall saw or jigsaw. Equip a drill with a long bit, and drill four locator holes through to the outside.

DUCT OPTIONS.

For maximum efficiency run the ducting directly to the outside. Usually that means going straight out the back. In some situations, however, you may need to run ducting up and over.

3 CUT THE SIDING.

On the outside hold the end cap up against the siding to make sure the locator holes are correct; you may need to enlarge or narrow the hole slightly. Cut the hole using a jigsaw or a reciprocating saw.

4 RUN THE CABLE.

Shut off the power. Run two-wire cable from a power source and through the small hole in the wall. Strip the sheathing, and clamp the cable to the range hood's housing.

5 INSTALL THE END CAP AND DUCT.

Cut the duct so it will reach the fan, and attach it to the end cap by driving screws and wrapping with professional-quality duct tape. Run a bead of caulk around the hole, and insert the duct through the hole. Press the end cap against the wall and drive screws to secure it.

6 ATTACH THE HOUSING.

Install the damper unit onto the housing. Position the housing and slide it so the duct fits over the damper unit. Drive four screws up through the housing and into the cabinet to secure it.

7 WIRE THE FAN.

Reassemble the range hood. In the fixture's junction box, connect the ground wires. Splice the white lead to the white wire and the black lead to the black wire. Tuck the wires in, and replace the coverplate.

After you've installed solid locks on your doors and outdoor lighting (see pages 96–97, 99), the next step toward a safer home is to add some electric security devices. Home centers often do not carry a wide choice of these products, but a visit to an electronics store or the Internet will reveal an array of possible devices.

The doorbell intercom on this page runs via your existing doorbell wires, and the intruder alert system on the opposite page is wireless, making both of these solutions easy to install.

INTERCOM OPTIONS

If you do not have functioning doorbell wires, consider a wireless intercom system. The intercom at the door communicates with one or more intercoms located anywhere in the house. You can also set up the system so the various indoor intercoms can communicate with each other.

Another system connects to telephone lines so when a person at the door pushes the button, your phones ring. You can pick up any phone and talk to the intercom.

YOU'LL NEED

TIME: About 1 hour for a doorbell intercom; several hours to install an alert system with 7 or 8 sensing devices.

SKILLS: No special skills required.

TOOLS: Screwdriver, drill.

1 INSTALL THE DOOR-BELL MODULE.

Remove the doorbell button and disconnect the wires. Clip the wires so they cannot slip back down the hole. Fasten the mounting bracket. Attach the bell wires to the terminal screws on the back of the doorbell module, and mount the module.

2 CONNECT TO THE TRANSFORMER.

Locate the existing doorbell transformer in your home (see page 54). Transfer the wires from its terminals to the new AC adapter that comes with the system. Plug the adapter into the nearest 120-volt receptacle. This links the doorbell module to the circuit that will carry the signal to the intercom monitor.

3 DISCONNECT THE CHIME OR BELL.

Take off the doorbell or chime cover. Unscrew the terminal screws and remove the wires. Twist the bare ends of the wires together, and cover the splice with a small wire nut. Because you will no longer need it, remove the doorbell.

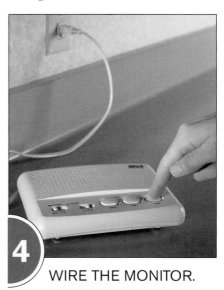

4 WIRE THE MONITOR.

Choose a location for the intercom monitor and fasten it to the wall with the screws provided. Then hang the unit in place and plug its cord into a receptacle.

WIRELESS SECURITY SYSTEM.

You can install a wireless security system for far less than it costs to have the pros do it. A typical console has 10 zones of wireless protection. Each zone is controlled by a single sensor, which may be a door/window sensor, a contact sensor, a motion detector, or a glass break detector. When a sensor is activated, a loud siren sounds. You can set the console for protection while you are at home or away. A keychain remote control allows you to turn the alarm on or off as you enter or leave the house. A rechargeable backup battery provides power when the electricity is off.

INSTALL A DOOR/WINDOW SENSOR.

Place the small part of the sensor on the door or window, and position the larger portion on the wall so that the two parts are aligned when the door or window is closed. Attach by driving screws.

GLASS BREAK DETECTOR.

Use this unit where an intruder may enter by breaking the glass—for example, a large first-floor window or a sliding glass door. It attaches to the glass via a suction cup.

MOTION DETECTOR.

This unit triggers the alarm when it senses motion. Install it about 3 feet above the floor near a main or rear entrance or in a hallway.

Electric cable often does not run in a straight line. Instead it zigzags from one outlet to another in a circuit. Sharp turns and long trips do not bother electricity. You can snake cable up and down walls, along or across joists, and around obstructions without impeding the flow of electrons.

In this home two general-purpose 120-volt circuits enter through the bottom plate of the stud wall and travel around perimeter walls to receptacle outlets. Two others go up into the ceiling for lighting, and a 240-volt circuit follows along a floor joist to serve an electric stove receptacle.

Saving money by planning

Even though electricity isn't affected by bends and detours, cable is priced by the foot, and extra feet can add up fast—in extra labor as well as materials. So to be economical keep your runs as short and direct as possible.

In new work that's not too difficult. In this illustration of a well-planned new home, most of the cables travel directly to their destinations. The plan saved money by installing the dryer outlet near the service panel, minimizing the amount of heavier, more costly cable needed for its 240-volt circuit.

The plan also saved the electrician time because there was no need for many bends in the conduit to carry the wire through exposed locations. The cable for the 240-volt receptacle for the electric stove, for example, takes as direct a path as possible along the basement sill plate.

Drawing up your plan

In planning an electrical layout, especially if you'll be running more than one circuit, draw a floor plan of your home to scale, then mark the routes the cable will travel. See page 34 for an example of circuits planned for the kitchen and family room, which are two of the more complex areas of a home.

To estimate how much cable you'll need, measure the distances involved and add 10 percent for bends, unexpected detours, and waste. Be sure to add in another 6 to 8 inches to make connections each time cable enters or leaves a junction or outlet box.

Working in finished spaces

If you plan to fish through finished walls and ceilings, be prepared to use more cable than you would if the framing were exposed.

You'll also have to do some detective work. Because cutting holes in walls and patching afterward takes so much time and effort, saving cable is a low priority when wiring in finished space. Search out the path that involves the least damage to your walls and offers the greatest ease in running the cable.

Your first task is to determine exactly what's in the space where you want to run the cable. If it's an exterior wall, for instance, there will probably be insulation, which makes fishing more difficult.

In addition many older homes have fire blocking that spans the studs about halfway up the wall. If faced with these barriers, you will have to notch the wall surface at those points. See pages 140–143 for tips on running cable in finished spaces.

Switch

Outdoor receptacle

240-volt circuit for electric stove

General purpose circuits

Service panel

Junction box

240-volt circuit for electric dryer

Bottom plate

Branch circuit

Adding a new circuit to your home's service panel is an advanced project and you may want to call in a professional—especially if your service panel is already crowded. Begin by seeing if you can add to an existing circuit. If not, then make sure the service can be expanded. Look for an amperage rating on the main fuse, main circuit breaker, or disconnect switch. Older 60-amp service can't be easily upgraded; call an electrician. Newer 100-amp service may have enough reserve to handle a new circuit or two, and 150- or 200-amp service usually has plenty of capacity.

YOU'LL NEED

TIME: 3 hours after running the cable to the service panel.

SKILLS: Understanding of electrical principles, general electrical skills.

TOOLS: Voltmeter, basic electrician's tools.

2 ESTIMATE CAPACITY NEEDED.

If you can't add to an existing circuit, check the chart at right for the capacity your new circuit likely needs. Rooms such as living rooms and bedrooms with about 10 light or receptacle outlets require only 15-amp capacity. Ideally you should have one general-purpose circuit for every 500 square feet of living space. Some local codes require that lighting and receptacles be on separate general-purpose circuits.

The kitchen is appliance-intensive and needs at least two 20-amp circuits. A bathroom gets by on one 15-amp circuit protected by a ground fault circuit interrupter. Circuits for the garage, laundry room, and workshop need 15- to 20-amp capacity.

1 ADD TO A CIRCUIT.

Different circuits have different capacities. If your need for extra capacity is modest, such as a few extra receptacles for a bedroom, see if you can add to a general-purpose or small-appliance circuit. (Never add on to a heavy-duty, single-use circuit). Figure the entire circuit load by totaling the demand of the appliances and fixtures (see page 34). Then check the chart at right to see if the demand is within a safe capacity. The safe capacity of a circuit, as prescribed by the National Electric Code, is 20 percent less than maximum capacity.

CIRCUIT CAPACITY

Circuit rating	Maximum capacity	Safe capacity
15 amps	1,800 watts	1,440 watts
20 amps	2,400 watts	1,920 watts
25 amps	3,000 watts	2,400 watts
30 amps	3,600 watts	2,880 watts

CIRCUIT NEED SELECTOR

Location	Circuits
Living and dining rooms, bedrooms, hallways, finished basements	A 15-amp general-purpose circuit for each 500 square feet. Separate circuits for lights and receptacles may be required by code. For a room air-conditioner, install a small-appliance circuit.
Kitchen	At least two 20-amp small-appliance circuits and a 15-amp lighting circuit. An electric range needs a 240-volt circuit. A microwave oven may need its own circuit.
Bathroom	A 20-amp receptacle circuit; lights must be on a different circuit.
Garage	A 15- or 20-amp general-purpose circuit (depending on tools and machinery, if any) with GFCI protection.
Laundry	A 20-amp small-appliance circuit for the washer and a gas dryer. An electric dryer needs a 240-volt circuit.
Workshop	A 20-amp GFCI circuit; for larger shops, run two 20-amp circuits or a separate circuit for lighting.
Outdoors	One 20-amp GFCI circuit.

3 CHECK THE TOTAL SERVICE CAPACITY.

Now that you know what additional circuit capacity you'll need, can your service capacity handle it? If you add up the amperage ratings for all the circuit breakers or fuses, plus the circuits you want to add, you may discover that the total equals or even exceeds the amperage rating of your service panel. Does that mean you can't add new circuits?

Not likely. Few, if any, of the circuits ever work at full amperage capacity. And some of your electrical fixtures and appliances never run at the same time—a furnace blower and an air-conditioner, for example. That's why codes allow you to derate your service capacity. Derating is a standardized reduction used when computing service capacity. The chart shows a derating calculation for a 2,000-square-foot house with 100-amp service, five small-appliance circuits, and two heavy-duty circuits.

In assigning wattage values, don't count each general-purpose circuit. Instead use 3 watts per square foot of house area. Small-appliance circuits rate at 1,500 watts each. Use the full wattage rating for heavy-duty circuits. If two items never run simultaneously, ignore the one that draws less. Rate only the first 10,000 watts of the total at full value, then calculate 40 percent of the remainder. Divide the total by 240 volts. The answer, 64.2 amps, shows that the system could accommodate more circuits.

DERATING SERVICE CAPACITY

Formula		Compute	
Add		The first 10,000 watts at 100 percent	10,000 W
General-purpose circuits (square footage x 3 watts)	6,000 W	The remaining 13,500 watts at 40 percent	+ 5,400 W
Small-appliance circuits (number x 1,500 watts)	7,500 W	Derated total	15,400 W
Heavy-duty circuits (total of appliance nameplate ratings in watts)	10,000 W	**Divide**	
Total:	23,500 W	The total derated wattage by voltage	/ 240 V
		Derated amperage	64.2 A

4 CHECK FOR ROOM IN THE BOX.

Double-pole breaker

Tandem breaker

Single-pole breaker

Half-size breaker

Once you've decided the type and capacity of your new circuit, see if you have room for it in your service panel. If your panel has circuit breakers, you might find a blank space or two.

(Unbroken knockouts on the panel indicate space for a breaker underneath.) If there isn't room you may be able to double up two circuits by replacing an existing breaker with a tandem breaker. In a fuse box you might find an unused terminal and socket that could work. More likely you'll have to add a secondary fuse box called a subpanel; consult with a professional.

ADDING MAJOR CIRCUITS

INSTALL A NEW CIRCUIT.

Shut off the power to the box. Before working on the box, work backward from the new electrical installation. Mount boxes, connect them with cable, and run wiring back to the service panel (see pages 132–155) in what the pros call a "home run." Allow yourself plenty of cable for running wires around the perimeter of the service panel when you install the new breaker.

Your home may have a main disconnect switch, which shuts off power to the service panel. It may be outdoors near the meter. If you have a main disconnect switch, shut it off; now there will be no power in the panel.

If you have no main disconnect, shut off the main breaker. Use a voltage detector to confirm that power is absent in the wires leading to the individual breakers. Work carefully, however, because power is present in the wires that lead to the main breaker.

CAUTION

LIVE CABLES

Remember that the main breaker or main fuse in a service panel does not de-energize the main power cables coming into the box. If you cannot shut off power to the service panel, work carefully, or call the power company to disconnect your service temporarily.

OUTDOOR SHUTOFF SWITCHES

An indoor service panel more than 5 feet from the meter requires an outdoor shutoff switch. If you have an outdoor shutoff switch, it's a good idea to keep it secured with a lock. Otherwise anyone passing through your backyard can easily turn off the power to your entire house.

RUN CABLE INTO THE SERVICE PANEL.

Remove a knockout plug at a convenient location. Install a cable clamp into the knockout hole. Hold the cable up to the panel to estimate how much wire you will need to run around the perimeter and to the new breaker location, and strip more sheathing than you need. Thread the exposed wires through the cable clamp, and tighten the clamp.

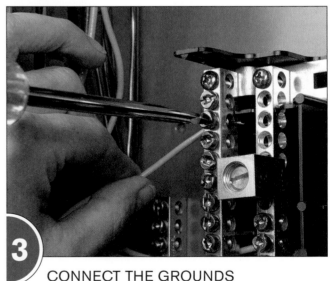

CONNECT THE GROUNDS AND NEUTRALS.

Some panels have one bus bar for the neutrals and a separate bar for the grounds; on other panels, you connect both neutrals and grounds to the same bar. Route the ground wire to an open terminal, cut it to fit, poke it into the terminal, and tighten the setscrew. Do the same for the neutral wire, but strip the wire end before inserting.

4 · HOOK THE HOT WIRE.

Route the hot wire to the location of the new breaker and cut it to fit, taking care that the wire will run neatly and stay at the perimeter of the panel as much as possible. Strip ½ inch of insulation, poke the wire into the breaker, and tighten the setscrew.

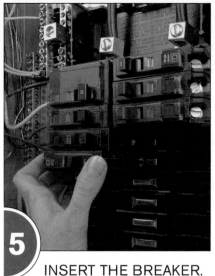

5 · INSERT THE BREAKER.

Examine nearby breakers to be sure you know how they attach. Push one side of the breaker fully onto one side of the hot bus bar, then push the other side. The breaker should be aligned with its neighbors.

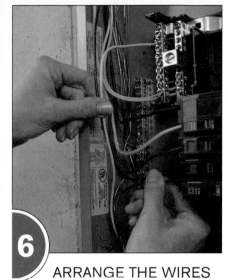

6 · ARRANGE THE WIRES AND TEST.

Double check that none of the wires crosses a hot bar. As far as possible arrange the wires neatly in the panel. Restore power, and test all the electrical outlets that are connected to the new circuit. Label the breaker (see page 35).

HOOK UP THE NEW BREAKERS.

Punch out the center from a convenient knockout on the circuit panel box. If needed, pry out one or more of the knockout's concentric rings to make a hole the size of the cable connector you'll be using.

Strip the cable sheathing, allowing for enough wire to reach the neutral bus bar as well as the blank space where you'll install the new breaker. Connect the cable to the box. Inside the service panel, run the white and ground wires to the neutral bus bar. (No ground wire is used if you are using conduit or BX.) For a 120-volt circuit, attach the black or red wire to the terminal of a single-pole breaker. To finish the job, simply clip the breaker onto one of the hot bus bars.

Some 240-volt appliances, such as water heaters, do not require a third neutral wire. For this type, connect two hot wires to a two-pole breaker (twice as wide as a single-pole breaker), and attach the ground wire to the neutral bus bar.

Most 240-volt circuits run a white, neutral wire and are sometimes called 120/240-volt circuits. Connect the two hot wires to the two-pole breaker and the white wire to the neutral bus bar. GFCI breakers install somewhat differently (see page 77).

DOUBLE-POLE BREAKER.

To install a new 240-volt circuit, consult with a professional electrician and check local codes for the correct type of cable and the correct breaker for your situation. Work especially carefully because 240 volts is enough to kill an adult. You will need a double-wide space in the panel to accommodate the 240-volt breaker. Shut off power, and run the cable in a home run from the outlet box to the panel. Take special care to clamp the cable securely. Connect the ground and neutral wire as described above. Connect two wires to the breaker, and snap the breaker into place. Restore power, and test.

Tools
AND MATERIALS

Electrical work is not difficult, but it must be done correctly. Be sure to get the right tools and materials so your installations will be safe and durable. In almost every case the same tools and materials used and installed by professional electricians are readily available for do-it-yourselfers.

Household wiring projects call for only a modest collection of inexpensive tools. Don't hesitate to spend a bit more for professional-quality tools, which usually make the work go more smoothly and are less likely to damage wires and devices.

Keep basic electrical tools together in a kit so you can easily grab the ones you need. An electrician's tool belt is ideal; just strap it on and you're ready to work.

Be sure the materials you purchase meet or exceed code requirements in your area. A local home center or hardware store will usually carry the correct materials. Sometimes even neighboring towns have different code requirements, so double-check with your building department before beginning any work. Switches, receptacles, and fixtures usually do not pose code issues; boxes and cable often do.

For extra peace of mind, don't just meet code; exceed it. If codes allow you to run exposed NM cable through a garage or basement, consider running armored cable or even conduit to be sure that it will not get damaged.

INFUSE A ROOM WITH WARMTH

The warm, yellow-tinted hue of incandescent light bulbs contrasts nicely with wood tones and green walls. A skylight provides light during the day, and recessed fixtures are positioned to take over when the sun goes down.

HIGHLIGHT WITH TRACK LIGHTING

The versatility of track lighting is on display in this loft family room. Some are trained on the textured block wall, where they make it look much warmer than the same material to the left. Others are pointed in various directions to provide both general illumination and focused lighting for a reader seated in a chair.

PLAN FOR APPLIANCES

Older microwaves were heavy electrical users that required their own circuits. Most modern microwaves do not pull nearly as much amperage and can be plugged into a receptacle on a circuit that supplies another small appliance or two.

WIRE A BEDROOM RETREAT

Wall sconces with swiveling arms and focused lights allow one partner to read while the other snoozes. A stereo system with speakers located high on the wall fills the room with generous sound. The control for the music system is just above the light switch.

ESSENTIAL TOOLS

You may be tempted to purchase an arsenal of expensive specialized tools for the projects in this book. However the basic tool kit shown on these pages will do just fine for most repairs and installations.

Lineman's pliers are a must. They have two flat surfaces that grab firmly and make it easy to neatly twist wires together for a solid electrical splice. You can also use them to cut wires. Use **long-nose** pliers to bend wires into the loops required when connecting to terminals. **Side-cutting pliers** (or diagonal cutters) make it easy to snip wires in tight places and are ideal for snipping sheathing from cable. A **utility knife** is useful for stripping NM cable sheathing and for cleaning up stripping jobs.

To strip wires use a **combination stripper**, which can also cut wire and bend it into loops. Buy one that has a self-opening spring; without this spring, stripping is much more laborious.

Use **screwdrivers** made for electrical work. They have insulating rubber grips that protect against shock. Buy sizes #1 and #2 of both slot and phillips types. A **rotary screwdriver** quickly drives or removes the little screws that anchor devices and coverplates.

Have at least one **voltage tester,** which tells you if power is present. A **neon voltage tester** is the simplest type. A **multilevel tester** works for standard 120- and 240-volt circuits as well as for low-voltage wiring for door chimes, a thermostat, and the like.

A **continuity tester** quickly tells you whether a device or fixture wiring or the circuitry is damaged. Just plug a **receptacle analyzer** into a receptacle and it will test for voltage, grounding, and polarization. Always buy good-quality testers to ensure accuracy.

Lineman's pliers

Combination stripper

Long-nose pliers

Side-cutting pliers

Rotary screwdriver

Screwdrivers

Neon voltage tester

Multilevel tester

Receptacle
analyzer

Voltage
tester

Utility knife

Continuity tester

SPECIALIZED TOOLS

If you will be running new cable or tackling other advanced projects, these tools are invaluable. Whenever you find that a new tool would make the job go more smoothly, it is almost always a good idea to buy or borrow that tool.

Running cable usually means drilling lots of holes, so you'll need a high-quality **drill** and a good collection of bits. Have several **spade bits** on hand, because they burn out easily. To drill deep holes, either use long bits or buy a bit extension.

For running cable through finished walls and ceilings, or for pulling wires through conduit, get a pair of **fish tapes.** A **fishing drill bit** can drill holes and then pull cable through studs or joists, eliminating the need to cut holes in the wall or ceiling.

Use a **hacksaw** to cut metal conduit or to nick armored sheathing prior to stripping. You can also use an **armored cable cutter** for this purpose. Cut metal conduit with a **tubing cutter** and bend it with a **conduit bender.**

A simple **drywall saw** is the tool of choice when cutting into finished walls or ceilings. (A power saw, such as a reciprocating saw, will cut more easily, but you might not notice if you run into a hidden cable or pipe.) A **flat prybar** helps you remove molding with minimal damage.

A **two-part circuit finder** makes it easy to determine which devices are on which circuit breaker. Use a **multitester** for repairs to appliances where you need to know the exact amounts of low voltage. If your house has cartridge fuses, buy a **fuse puller.**

Fishing drill bit

Fish tape

Fuse puller

Spade bit

Drill

Tubing cutter

Conduit bender

Armored cable cutter

Multitesters
Analog meter, above,
Digital, below

Hacksaw

Voltage detector

Drywall saw

Flat prybar

Two-part circuit finder

Conduit reamer

CHOOSING SWITCHES

Manufacturers offer an assortment of switches. To begin with, you have a choice of colors. The most readily available are brown, ivory, and white. But the differences extend far beyond appearance.

For most of your needs, you'll probably choose a **single-pole toggle,** which is available for a low price. "Toggle" simply refers to a switch with a lever that flips up and down.

Three-way and **four-way** switches control a light from two or three separate locations. To learn about wiring them, see pages 89–92.

If you want to add a switch without putting in a larger box, a **double** switch may be the solution. It takes up the same amount of space as a single switch.

A **rocker** switch functions the same way as a standard toggle switch and is slightly easier to use.

A **dimmer** switch allows you to adjust lighting levels to suit your needs. A sliding dimmer brightens the light as you slide it upward. The rotary type comes in two versions. One version turns lights on or off with a push; the light level changes by turning the knob. The other type dims the light by rotating the knob counterclockwise until it turns off.

Single-pole toggle   Three-way   Four-way

Double   Rocker

LOOK FOR THE UL SYMBOL

The UL symbol means that electrical materials have been checked for any defects by Underwriters Laboratories, an independent testing organization. Local codes may prohibit using items not UL-listed.

Sliding dimmer   Rotary dimmer

SELECTING SPECIAL SWITCHES

Of the many available switches built to suit special needs, the ones on this page are some of the most common. Take a trip to a home center or a lighting store, and you may find the switch that does exactly what you want. To find out how to install these switches, see pages 74–75.

If you have power tools or other devices that you don't want children to play with, consider installing a **tamperproof** switch. Operated only with a key, it can be wired to control the receptacle connecting the equipment.

For security in your backyard, or to have a light automatically greet you as you approach your house, choose a **motion-sensor security** switch. Its wide-angle infrared beam detects motion and turns the light on automatically. With most units you can choose how long the light will stay on.

A **pilot-light** switch has a little bulb that glows when power flows through the switch. Use it when a fixture or appliance is out of sight. These switches often control closet lights, attic exhaust fans, basement lights, and garage lights.

If you need to squeeze both a switch and an outlet into a single box, use a **switch/receptacle.** Also use this switch to easily add a receptacle to a room. This switch can be wired so the receptacle is live all the time or wired so the switch controls the receptacle.

A **programmable** switch comes with digital controls and can be programmed to turn lights on and off up to four times a day. This type of switch is useful for security and deterring burglars when you are away from home.

A **time-delay** switch has a dial that can be set to leave a fixture running for up to 60 minutes. Use one for a vent fan, space heater, heat lamp, or garage light.

Programmable   Motion-sensor   Timer   Socket receiver

Time-delay   Pilot-light   Switch/Receptacle   Keychain remote switch

CHOOSING RECEPTACLES

A standard duplex receptacle has two outlets for receiving plugs. Each outlet has a long (neutral) slot, a shorter (hot) slot, and a half-round grounding hole. This ensures that the plug will be polarized and grounded (see page 26).

Receptacles are rated for maximum amps. A **20-amp grounded receptacle** has a T-shaped neutral slot; use it only on 20-amp circuits. For most purposes a **15-amp grounded receptacle** is sufficient. When replacing a receptacle in an ungrounded outlet box, install a **15-amp ungrounded receptacle,** intended only for use in older homes without ground wires in the circuits. Use a three-pronged plug adapter on an ungrounded receptacle only if the wall-plate screw is grounded (see page 33 to test this). The switch in a combination **switch/receptacle** can be hooked up to control the receptacle. A **20-amp single grounded receptacle** makes it nearly impossible to overload a critical circuit. For outdoors, in basements, or within 6 feet of a water fixture, install **ground fault circuit interrupter (GFCI) receptacles** (see page 77). Select a **240-volt receptacle** based on the appliance amperage rating. Plugs required for appliances of 15, 20, 30, and 50 amps will have different prong configurations.

Essential receptacles

15-amp ungrounded

20-amp grounded

15-amp grounded

Switch/Receptacle

Specialized receptacles

GFCI receptacle

30-amp 120/240-volt wall-mounted

50-amp 120/240-volt

Duplex with 20-amp 240V for air conditioner

20-amp 120V grounded single

50-amp 120/240-volt grounded

> ## ▼ CAUTION
>
> ### REPLACE, DON'T CHANGE
>
> Replace a receptacle with one that is just like the old one. Change types only if you are certain that the wiring is suitable. Do not replace an ungrounded outlet with a grounded one unless you know the box is grounded.

CHOOSING WIRE AND CABLE

Wire, cord, and cable (generically referred to as "conductors") are the pathways along which electricity travels. Wire is a solid strand of metal encased in insulation. Cord is a group of small strands surrounded by insulation. Cable is made of two or more wires wrapped in a protective sheathing of metal or plastic.

Most local codes allow you to use nonmetallic sheathed cable (NM cable) inside walls, floors, and other places where it can't be damaged and won't get wet. Information printed on the sheathing tells you what is inside. The top example, right, has two 14-gauge wires plus a bare ground wire, and is referred to as "14/2 G" cable ("G" for ground). Cable marked "14/3" has three wires plus a ground wire. Armored cable contains wires wrapped in a flexible metal sheathing. Older armored cable, called BX, has a thin bonding wire but no actual ground wire; the sheathing itself is used to conduct the ground. Modern MC armored cable has a green-insulated ground wire. Underground feed (UF) cable is watertight, with the sheathing molded around the wire. Many municipalities permit this for underground lines.

Different gauge wires carry different amounts of electricity—14-gauge carries a maximum of 15 amps, 12-gauge carries up to 20 amps, and 10-gauge wire handles up to 30 amps. Unsheathed wires are pulled through flexible or rigid conduit. Flexible metal conduit, or Greenfield, looks like armored cable but doesn't contain wires. Using Greenfield involves cutting it to length, pulling the wires through, and installing the completed pieces. With rigid conduit you pull the wires through after it's installed (see pages 152–155). Doorbells and other low-voltage circuits typically use 18-gauge wire.

2-wire NM cable

3-wire NM cable

MC cable

BX cable

Bonding wire

UF Cable

10-gauge wire

12-gauge wire

14-gauge wire

18-gauge wire

WHAT THE COLORS MEAN

Color	Function
White	Neutral, carrying power back to the service panel.
Black	Hot, carrying power from the service panel.
Red and other colors	Also hot, color-coded to help identify which circuit they are on.
White and black tape	A white wire that is being used as a hot wire.
Bare or green	A ground wire.

CHOOSING BOXES

An electrical box's primary function is to house electrical connections. Those connections might be to a switch, a receptacle, the leads of a light fixture, or other sets of wires.

Electrical codes require that all wire connections or cable splices be inside an approved metal or plastic box. And every box must be accessible—you cannot bury it inside a wall. This protects your home from the danger of fire and makes it easier to inspect and upgrade your wiring in the future.

Codes govern how many connections you're allowed to make within a box, depending on its size. If you must make more connections, you have to use a larger box.

There are boxes to suit almost any depth of wall or ceiling, to support heavy fixtures such as ceiling fans, and for remodeling work and new construction. If, for instance, you'll be pulling cables through a finished wall, you can choose from a number of retrofit boxes that can be mounted with minimal damage to the wall.

Boxes for switches and receptacles serve as the workhorses in any electrical installation. Some of the metal ones can be "ganged" into double, triple, or larger multiples by removing one side and linking them together. Most codes accept switch/receptacle boxes made of plastic, but they can't be ganged. If you are using conduit, Greenfield, or BX, you must use metal boxes to ground the system.

Utility boxes are surface-mounted in basements and garages to hold switches or receptacles. Boxes for fixtures or junctions may support lighting fixtures or split circuits into separate branches.

CHOOSING THE CORRECT BOX SIZE

Type of Box	Size in Inches (Height × Width × Depth)	Maximum Number of Wires Allowed in Box		
		14-gauge	12-gauge	10-gauge
Switch/ Receptacle	3×2×1½	3	3	3
	3×2×2	5	4	4
	3×2×2¼	5	4	4
	3×2×2½	6	5	5
	3×2×2¾	7	6	5
	3×2×3½	9	8	7
Utility	4×2⅛×1½	5	4	4
	4×2⅛×1⅞	6	5	5
	4×2⅛×2⅛	7	6	5
Fixture/ Junction	4×1¼ round or octagonal	6	5	5
	4×1½ round or octagonal	7	6	6
	4×2⅛ round or octagonal	10	9	8
	4×1¼ square	9	8	7
	4×1½ square	10	9	8
	4×2⅛ square	15	13	12
	4¹¹⁄₁₆×1½ square	14	13	11
	4¹¹⁄₁₆×2⅛ square	21	18	16

BOX CAPACITY

Overcrowd a box and you risk damaging wire connectors, piercing insulation, and cracking a switch or receptacle, any of which could cause a short. That is why codes spell out how many wires you can install in a box.

The chart above gives standard requirements. Other items may add to the total number of wires a box can hold. As you count wires, keep in mind these rules:

■ Don't count fixture leads (the wires that are connected to the fixture).

■ Count a wire that enters and leaves without a splice as one.

■ Count each cable clamp, stud, or hickey inside the box as one wire.

■ Count each receptacle or switch as one.

■ Count grounding wires entering a box as one, but do not count grounding wires that begin and end in the box.

NEW-WORK SWITCH/RECEPTACLE BOXES

These boxes are designed for quick installation when the framing is exposed. They all have built-in gauges to make it easy to install them flush with the surface of the finished wall.

4×4 box with nailing spurs.

Metal box with nailing bracket. Side removes so additional box can be added on.

2×4 box with front-nailing bracket.

Side "W" bracket holds box away from the stud.

2×4 plastic box with front-nailing bracket.

2×4 plastic box with 16d nails.

4×4 plastic box with nails angled for easy fastening.

RETROFIT SWITCH/RECEPTACLE BOXES

When installing new electrical service where the walls are finished, use boxes designed to minimize damage to the wall. If the special clips do not work, you may be able to attach the boxes to framing pieces with screws driven through holes inside the boxes.

Metal "wings" slip behind wall; flaps fold over the box.

Tightening the screw pulls the pointed flanges forward.

Screw-in clamps move forward to hold box in place.

2×4 plastic box with plastic "ears" that swing out and forward as screws tighten.

4×4 plastic box with plastic "ears."

NEW-WORK FIXTURE/JUNCTION BOXES

New-work wiring refers to work done on a freshly framed wall. With no drywall or plaster in the way, it is easy to install ceiling fixture boxes that are solid enough to hold a heavy chandelier or a fan. Remember that all junction boxes must remain accessible—never cover them with drywall.

Telescoping brackets allow you to position these boxes anywhere between joists.

Metal octagonal box requires framing behind it if it will support a heavy fixture.

Round plastic fixture box has a bracket with sharp points so you can quickly tap it in place, then secure it with screws.

Octagonal junction box with side bracket nailed to framing.

RETROFIT FIXTURE/JUNCTION BOXES

Retrofitting and adding new wiring to old walls is challenging. Often it's not easy to secure a fixture box when there's drywall or plaster in the way. For heavy ceiling fixtures use a brace bar that can be slipped into the hole and expanded from joist to joist (see page 81).

A shallow box like this is sometimes needed in older homes with plaster walls.

USE NEW INSTALLATION BOXES IN UNFINISHED SPACES

Most homes have areas where the walls or ceilings are unfinished, such as basements, attics, and garages. Whenever you are adding improvements to these areas, or adding junction boxes that will serve existing circuits, use new installation boxes. Use metal boxes with metal coverplates, even if you are using nonmetallic sheathed cable, because they may get bumped. Plastic boxes will crack.

"Wings" come forward as you tighten the screws, clasping the box to the plaster or drywall.

Most retrofitting starts with standard junction boxes located in accessible areas.

SPECIALIZED BOXES

Wiring can be full of surprises. If you run into an unusual situation, chances are there is a specialized box that can help. Here are a few of the many boxes designed to cope with tight spaces, new framing materials, and changes in wall-surface depth.

Weatherproof die-cast aluminum box can be surface-mounted for outdoor fixtures.

Metal studs are increasingly popular for house construction. Box mounts on either side of a metal stud.

Box mounts on the flat side of a metal stud.

A screw on the wall clip lets you adjust the depth of the box to account for the thickness of tile or paneling.

1¼-inch-thick box fits shallow wall cavities.

Ceiling box slips onto a joist and is strong enough to support a ceiling fan.

BOX ACCESSORIES

Box accessories are numerous. Some, such as mudrings, should be installed before applying the wall surface. Others cap off boxes for special needs.

Weatherproof coverplate for an exterior GFCI receptacle.

Knockout filler plugs a knockout hole that is not being used.

Extender ring brings a fixture box out ½ inch—especially useful when drywall is added over plaster.

Blank plate and one- and two-device "mudrings" for placing receptacles in large boxes.

Blank plate covers an octagonal or round junction box.

Weathertight housings for an outdoor box: blank, 1-fixture, and 2-fixture.

Box extender slides inside the box.

Wiring
TECHNIQUES

**INSTALL
PRODUCTIVE
WORK LIGHTING**
Plan office lighting
with care so that
work surfaces are
illuminated without
glaring in the eye of
a seated worker.
Here tiny lights are
recessed into
the undersides of
shelves and cabinets.

Safe electrical work starts with a clear understanding of the wiring system. Before you open a box, replace a fixture, run cable, or test any part of your system, read "Getting to Know Your System," beginning on page 16. Never begin a wiring project if you are unsure of what you are doing. If you run into a situation you don't understand, call in a professional.

Making sound wiring connections calls for a few simple techniques that can be learned in an hour or two. If you follow these steps correctly, your connections will remain secure and safe for many decades.

Sloppy connections will likely work. However, it is quite possible they will loosen in time, causing the wiring to function erratically and creating a dangerous situation.

If you use quality tools made for electrical work (see pages 118–121), it will be easy to produce professional connections. Working with household or carpentry tools will make the job difficult and slow.

While connecting wires, fixtures, and devices is relatively easy, running cable can be difficult. This is especially true if you need to run cable through finished walls and ceilings. This chapter shows many tips and techniques to help minimize damage to interior surfaces. Be aware, though, that in remodel wiring, you will likely spend most of your time cutting into drywall or plaster and patching it afterwards.

BRIGHTEN A HALLWAY OR ENTRYWAY

If wood paneling can be removed and reinstalled without damage, you can run electrical lines for new sconces with little difficulty.

To wire a room with unfinished walls, such as a basement remodeling or a room addition, you'll need boxes fastened to the framing. When attaching the boxes, be sure they protrude from the framing the same thickness as your drywall or paneling—usually ½ inch. Run cable from box to box and to the service panel.

After you've roughed in the wiring, but before you install the switches and receptacles, put up the drywall on the walls and ceiling. Finish and prime the surfaces, and install the devices in the boxes.

PLACING BOXES

In a typical room place switch boxes 48 to 50 inches above the floor, receptacles 12 to 16 inches above floor level. Check with local codes to see how many receptacles you will need. In most cases they must be placed so that no point along any wall is more than 6 feet from a receptacle. This means that you'll have to install at least one receptacle every 12 feet along the wall. For kitchens and bathrooms, special requirements apply.

YOU'LL NEED

TIME: About 3 hours for installing 10 boxes.

SKILLS: Basic carpentry skills.

TOOLS: Tape measure, hammer or drill with screwdriver bit.

NONMETALLIC HANDY BOX.

Many boxes have a series of gauging notches on their sides. Determine the thickness of the drywall and/or paneling you will be installing, and align the box to the appropriate notch as you attach it. A nail-up box like this one is the easiest to install.

GANGABLE BOXES.

These have detachable sides, so you can connect them together to form double- or triple-sized boxes. To attach the boxes without using special mounting hardware, drive screws or nails through the holes and into the framing.

L-BRACKET BOX.

Some L-bracket boxes adjust to suit the thickness of your wall material. Others accommodate only one thickness. Hold the box in position against the framing, and drive two nails or screws through the holes in the bracket.

UTILITY BOX.

Use a utility box and conduit or armored cable in an area where you don't need a finished appearance. If you're attaching boxes to masonry, use anchors or masonry screws.

ixture and junction boxes are easy to add in unfinished spaces. Install boxes so they will be flush with the finished surface of the ceiling or wall. Do not place any electrical box where it will be covered by drywall or paneling.

If there is a joist at the spot where you want the box, use a box with a hanger bracket or an **L-bracket**. This page shows various types available—some work from below, some work from above. These fasten to the joist with screws or nails. When fastening allow for the thickness of the ceiling material.

If you need to install a fixture box between joists, use a box with a **bar hanger**. Attach the ends of the brackets to the joists, and slide the box into the desired position.

Junction boxes protect wire connections or cable splices. Some junction boxes come with brackets. Others nail or screw to a joist, stud, or rafter.

Regardless of the type of box you're installing, always secure it with two fasteners. If the box will support a ceiling fan or other heavy fixture, make sure it's anchored securely to carry the load. If a box has been correctly mounted but still doesn't feel firm enough, add a framing piece and secure it to that as well.

Box with hanger bracket

L-bracket box

Box with bar hanger

4-inch octagonal junction box

Square junction box

OVERHEAD LIGHT PLACEMENT

One pleasing way to light a room is with recessed lights (see pages 68–69) or small fixtures. To plan for a group of symmetrically placed lights, make a map of your ceiling and experiment by drawing circles, each representing the area lit by a recessed fixture.

When you experiment with your design, try to arrange the lights so they are half as far from the walls as they are from each other. A pleasingly symmetrical pattern usually results. Start by arranging lights 6 feet apart and 3 feet from the walls. Avoid positioning them closer than 4 feet apart. Include any suspended or track lighting you need for task illumination or to accent an attractive area of the room.

Don't expect to achieve an arrangement that's perfectly symmetrical; few ceilings will allow for that. Also keep in mind that, with recessed lighting, you may not be able to put all the lights exactly where you want them because there will be joists in the way. In most cases a less-than-perfect arrangement will not be noticeable.

Installing electrical work is a greater challenge when the walls and ceilings are finished. Often patching and painting can take far more time than the electrical work itself! Plan the placement so you avoid making unnecessary holes.

Avoid contact with the framing wherever possible. Using special boxes designed for installation in finished space, you often can make a hole the size of the box and secure the box to the wall or ceiling surface.

Before you begin, plan how you're going to get cable to the new location (see pages 140–145).

YOU'LL NEED

TIME: About 30 minutes a box, not including running new wire.

SKILLS: Basic carpentry skills.

TOOLS: Keyhole saw, drill, hammer, screwdriver, utility knife.

1 DETERMINE BOX LOCATION.

Drill a small hole in the wall. Insert a bent wire and rotate it. If you hit something, you've probably found a stud. Drill 6 inches to one side. If you strike wood again, you may have hit a fire block. Drill another hole 3 inches higher or lower. Keep trying until you can rotate the bent wire freely.

2 TRACE AROUND BOX.

Some boxes come with a template that can be held against the surface and traced around. Otherwise use the box itself and center it on the hole you rotated the wire in. Make sure the template or box is plumb before you mark the outline.

3 CUT THE OPENING.

Carefully cut around the traced outline. If the surface is drywall, use a utility knife. If you are cutting into plaster walls, use a keyhole saw. If the plaster is crumbly, mask the outline with tape. For a wood-surfaced wall, drill a ¼-inch access hole in each corner and use a saber saw. Run cable (see pages 140–145).

4 FASTEN WITH SIDE CLAMPS …

Side-clamp boxes grip the wall from behind when you tighten the screws. Pull 8 inches of cable through the box and insert the box into the wall. Hold the box plumb as you tighten the clamps. Alternate from side to side as you work so the box seats evenly. Avoid overtightening the clamps.

OR TIGHTEN WING CLIPS.

Loosen the screw centered in the receptacle box until the wing bracket is completely extended from the back. Hold the wings against the body of the box and push the box into the hole. Tighten the screw until the box is firmly in place.

Box attached to framing

Bar hanger

2×4 support

WITH ACCESS FROM ABOVE.

A ceiling box supports a fixture, so it must be securely attached to the framing. If you are fortunate enough to have attic space above, the job can be done without damaging your ceiling. Mark the location of each box on the ceiling, and drive nails as reference points. Cut the hole for the box. If there is a nearby joist, attach an L-bracket box directly to it. If not, use a bar hanger or frame in a 2×4 support.

Old-work box

Pancake box

Bar hanger

WITH NO ACCESS FROM ABOVE.

If you cannot work from above, use one of these methods. For most light fixtures, which weigh less than 5 pounds, use an old-work box. Cut the hole, slip the box in, and tighten screws to clamp the box to the drywall or plaster. If a joist is in the way and you cannot move the box to the side, install a pancake box, which is screwed directly to the joist. To support a heavy fixture such as a chandelier or a fan, follow the instructions on pages 80–81 for installing a braced box. If the ceiling is damaged anyway, you may choose to cut out a rectangular section of ceiling and install a bar hanger box.

REPAIR THE CEILING.

After checking the electrical installation, patch the ceiling. With drywall you may be able to use the same piece you cut out. Nail the panel to the joists, and tape the seam with joint compound. For a plaster ceiling fill with patching compound.

Before making electrical connections, you must remove some of the sheathing that encases the three or four wires of the cable. You will also need to strip some of the insulation that coats the individual wires. Stripping techniques are easy but exercise care when removing sheathing in order to avoid damaging any of the underlying insulation. Also be careful to strip the insulation without nicking the copper wire—this would weaken it.

Instead of stripping the wires after the cable is pulled into the box, strip the wires before inserting them. That way if you make a mistake you can cut off the damaged portion and try again.

YOU'LL NEED

TIME: About 5 minutes or less.

SKILLS: Stripping wire.

TOOLS: Cable ripper, wire stripper, utility knife, side cutters, combination tool, lineman's pliers.

CAUTION

STRIP WIRE CAREFULLY

This job is simple, but it must be done with great care or you could end up with dangerous electrical shorts. If you think you may have accidentally damaged some insulation, cut the cable back to a place behind the potentially dangerous spot, and start again.

Another possible problem: If you cut into the copper wire while stripping the insulation, you can weaken the wire. This may cause it to break while you are making a connection later.

Stripping sheathing

1 SLIT THE SHEATHING.

The easiest way to remove plastic sheathing from nonmetallic sheathed cable is to use an inexpensive cable ripper. Slip 6 to 8 inches of cable into the ripper's jaws, squeeze, and pull. This slits open the sheathing without damaging the insulation of internal wires. The same job can be done with a knife, but you must be careful: Run the blade right down the middle so it doesn't strip insulation from the wires.

2 PEEL BACK THE SHEATHING.

Pull back the sheathing you have just slit as well as the paper wrapping or strips of thin plastic, if any. You'll find two or three separately insulated wires, as well as a bare ground wire.

3 CUT AWAY THE SHEATHING.

Cut off the sheathing and paper. Remove the slit sheathing with a pair of side cutters. Or use a knife, taking care to point the blade away from the wires.

Stripping wire

STRIP THE WIRE.

To strip insulation from wires, use a combination tool, which has separate holes for the different sizes of wires. Locate the wire in the correct hole, clamp down, give it a twist, and pull the tool away from you.

Use the same technique with an adjustable stripper. The advantage of this tool is that, once it is set correctly for the wire size, it is not necessary to look for the right hole every time. Stripping also can be

done with a utility knife, but be careful not to dig into the copper wire. Place the wire on a scrap piece of wood, hold the blade at a slight angle, and make several light slices.

Joining wires

JOINING SOLID WIRES.

Join solid wires by using a pair of lineman's pliers. Cross the two wires, grab both wires with the pliers, and twist clockwise. Both wires should twist—do not twist one wire around the other. Turn for several revolutions, but don't twist so tightly that the wires are in danger of breaking. Screw a wire nut onto the two wires (see page 138).

1 JOIN STRANDED TO SOLID WIRES.

Often a stranded wire (made of many thin wires) has to be spliced to a solid wire, as when hooking up a light fixture or dimmer switch. Because the stranded wire is more flexible, the two won't twist together. Wrap the stranded wire around the solid wire.

2 FOLD THE SOLID WIRE OVER.

Bend the solid wire so it clamps down on the stranded wire. Screw a wire nut onto the two wires, and wrap the connection with electrician's tape.

The final—and most gratifying—phase of an electrical installation comes when you tie all those wires together and attach them to the switches, light fixtures, and receptacles. Don't take shortcuts with wire connections and splices. Cap splices with wire connectors, and wrap tape around each connector. Make pigtails wherever they are needed instead of trying to connect two or more wires to a terminal. Finally don't overcrowd a box with too many wires (for limits, see the chart on page 126).

HOW MANY WIRES IN A CONNECTOR?

Wire connector	12-gauge wires	14-gauge wires
Red	2–4	2–5
Yellow	2–3	2–4
Orange	2	2–4

USING WIRE CONNECTORS.

To complete a splice of two or more wires, use wire connectors. These come in a variety of sizes. Select the size you need depending on how many wires you will connect as well as the thickness of the wires (see chart, left). Wire connectors firm up the splice and protect bare wires

better than tape. First twist the wires firmly together. Do not depend on the connector to do the joining. Twist the wire connector on, turning it by hand until it tightens firmly. As a final precaution wrap the connector clockwise with electrical tape, overlapping the wires.

1

CONNECT A WIRE TO A TERMINAL.

Strip the insulation from just enough wire to make a loop that will wrap around the terminal—about ¾ inch.

2

BEND THE END INTO A LOOP.

Form the wire into a loop using needle-nose pliers. It takes practice to make loops that lie flat under the terminal screw and are neither too big nor too small.

3

TIGHTEN THE SCREW.

Hook the wire clockwise around the terminal so tightening the screw will close the loop. A black wire goes to the brass screw, a white wire attaches to the silver terminal. Tighten the screw, but avoid overtightening, which can damage the device. If you do crack a device, replace it.

CONNECTING WIRES

Attach to terminals

BACKWIRED DEVICES

ATTACH MULTIPLE WIRES TO A TERMINAL WITH A PIGTAIL.

Never attach more than one wire to a terminal. Codes prohibit it, and it's unsafe because terminal screws are made to hold only one wire. The safe way to join many wires to a terminal is to cut a short piece of wire (about 4 inches), strip both ends, and splice it to the other wires as shown to form a pigtail.

... OR SOLDER A SPLICE.

Make sure local codes permit soldered connections; some codes require soldered splices, but they are more often prohibited for house wiring. Twist wires together so that one extends 1 inch beyond the splice. Heat the wires with a soldering iron, then touch lead-free, rosin-core solder to the wires. The solder should melt into the splice. Tape the soldered splice.

Many receptacles and switches have connection holes in the back. To make a connection, strip the wire (a stripping gauge often is provided, showing you how much insulation to remove) and poke it into the correct hole. On a receptacle the holes are marked for white and black wires. However, most professionals do not use these holes. Wires inserted this way are simply not as secure as those screwed to a terminal.

GROUNDING RECEPTACLES AND SWITCHES.

How you ground receptacles and switches depends on local codes as well as the type of box and cable. With older installations of flexible armored cable (BX), Greenfield, or metal conduit, the metal of the wiring casing and the metal of the box substitutes for the grounding wire. By attaching the device firmly to the box, you have grounded it. Modern codes, however, call for MC armored cable, which has a grounded wire (left), or a separate ground wire for conduit or Greenfield. Ideally, the ground wire should be attached to the box via a pigtail (middle). Use this technique with nonmetallic sheathed cable and metal boxes. In some older installations a ground wire is attached to a metal box using a clip that mounts to the side of the box (not shown). With nonmetallic boxes, connect the grounding wire directly to the device (right).

Do some detective work before running cable through finished walls and ceilings. As far as possible determine what's in the wall or ceiling cavity. Look for access from an unfinished attic floor or basement ceiling. Check to see if there is insulation or blocking in the way. Determine whether or not there is a way to run cable parallel to the joists and studs. Make as few holes as possible since patching walls and ceilings is often the most time-consuming part of running cable. Use patching plaster, drywall tape, and compound to fix any holes.

YOU'LL NEED

TIME: About 3 hours.

SKILLS: Drilling and patching.

TOOLS: Power drill, ¾- and 1-inch bits, fish tape, keyhole saw, utility knife, chisel, hammer, standard carpentry tools.

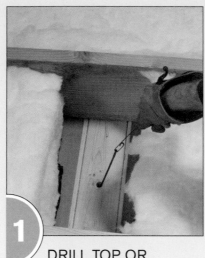

1 DRILL TOP OR BOTTOM PLATES...

If there is access from above or below, drill into the top or bottom plates of the wall frame. For a double plate or awkward angle, use a bit extension. After drilling the hole fish the cable to the box opening. If you hit fire blocking (horizontal pieces between the studs) see Step 4.

...OR CUT AN OPENING.

When there is no room for drilling through the plates from above or below, bore from the side instead. At the top of the wall, cut an opening to expose the single or double plate. At the bottom there will only be a single plate; remove the baseboard, and make the cutout ¾ inch above the floor.

2 DRILL THE HOLE.

Using a bit extension, bore into the bottom of the plate, angling toward the center. Bore slowly to avoid burning out the drill. Watch out for nails. Remember to wear goggles when working with power tools.

3 PUSH THE CABLE THROUGH.

Push the cable up or down to the box opening. Then loop it through the plate. Pulling cable through walls is a two-person job. One person tugs—not too hard or the sheathing might tear—from the attic or basement. The other coils cable and feeds it through the opening, taking care to avoid kinks and knots.

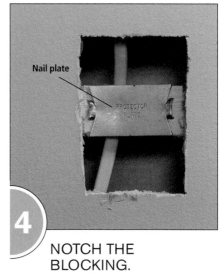

Nail plate

4 NOTCH THE BLOCKING.

To locate fire blocking slip a tape measure through the hole and push it until it strikes the blocking. Measure to that point and make an opening that straddles the blocking. Chisel a notch that is large enough to accommodate the cable easily. After you've run the cable, but before you patch the hole, install a nail plate.

SHORT RUNS OF CABLE.

Often the easiest way to fish cable is from a nearby receptacle. Before tapping into a receptacle, make sure you won't be overloading the circuit (see pages 112–113). Shut off the power. Remove the coverplate and see if the receptacle has a set of unused terminals. If it doesn't, add pigtails (see page 139) before reconnecting.

YOU'LL NEED

TIME: About 2 hours, not including wall patching.

SKILLS: Pulling wire and patching drywall or plaster.

TOOLS: Fish tape, keyhole saw, utility knife, standard carpentry tools.

1

OPEN THE BOX.

Disconnect the receptacle. Check for a cable clamp or other device that will attach the new cable to the box. If necessary remove a knockout with a hammer and screwdriver, and install a clamp.

2

CUT THE NEW OPENING.

Use a box as a template to mark the new outlet opening and cut it open with a utility knife or keyhole saw. Locate the new box in the same wall cavity as the source box if possible.

3

CONNECT FISH TAPES.

Thread one fish tape (or bent coat hanger) through the knockout hole and another through the new opening. Wiggle one or both until they hook together. Pull the tape from the existing box through the new opening. Strip some sheathing from the cable, hook the wires to the end of the fish tape and wrap with electrical tape.

4

PULL THE CABLE THROUGH.

Pull the cable through the new opening and into the old box. Connect the cable to the old box (see page 138), and install the new box (see page 134).

CUT NOTCHES

To run cable past a stud, notch the stud. Cut the wall covering across the stud. Save the cutout piece. Chisel a notch in the stud, lay in the cable, and install a nail plate to protect the cable. Patch the wall.

Nail plate

RUN CABLE BETWEEN JOISTS.

To minimize holes in the ceiling, run cable in the same direction as the joists. Where you must run the cable across joists, use a stud finder to locate the joists, and cut holes that are large enough to stick your arm through. Using a drill equipped with a long bit, bore holes through the joists and thread the cable through.

DRILL AND PULL WIRE WITH ONE TOOL.

A fishing bit allows you to run cable across joists or studs with half the holes. Drill through two joists or studs, and leave the bit in place. Attach the cable to the bit and pull it back through both holes.

RUNNING CABLE THROUGH THE BASEMENT

1 INSERT A LOCATOR WIRE.

To run wire down through a basement with an unfinished ceiling, pry off the base shoe or the baseboard. Drill a locator hole, and thread a straight wire down through the hole.

2 DRILL UP THROUGH THE WALL.

Go to the basement and find the locator wire. Drill a hole up through the center of the wall—about 2¼ inches from the wire for a 2×4 stud wall with ½-inch drywall.

3 RUN THE CABLE.

You may be able to have a helper poke the cable up through the hole in the basement and wiggle it; when you see it, grab it. Otherwise insert a fish tape down through the hole in the wall and the hole in the floor, attach the cable, and pull it up.

RUNNING CABLE BEHIND BASEBOARDS AND CASING

1 CUT A CHANNEL.

For safety run armored cable (MC) rather than nonmetallic cable (NM) whenever you are sneaking it behind a piece of molding. Remove a baseboard, and cut a strip of drywall or plaster that will be covered when you replace the baseboard.

2 DRILL HOLES OR CUT NOTCHES.

If there is room drill holes through the centers of the exposed studs. If space is tight use a reciprocating saw or a hand saw to cut notches in the studs. You will likely encounter nails as you do so. Trim the nails back so they cannot damage the cable.

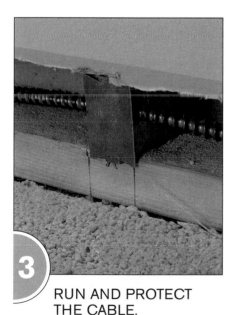

3 RUN AND PROTECT THE CABLE.

Feed the cable through the hole where it will access power and through the holes or notches in the studs. Protect the cable by installing nailing plates at each stud.

4 BRING CABLE TO THE NEW OUTLET.

If the hole for the new box is low enough, push the cable up through the wall to the hole. To pull the cable up to a higher opening, use a fish tape.

RUN CABLE ALONG JAMB.

To run cable around a door, carefully remove the casing. Push the cable into the space between the jamb and the wall material, notching where necessary. If the jamb is tight against a stud, drill a hole in or notch the stud, thread the cable through the hole or notch, and run it up or down through the wall.

If you're working on a new addition, or if you've gutted a room and removed the old walls, running cable will be much easier. Begin by installing the electrical boxes. Place all the receptacles and switches at uniform height (12 to 18 inches from the floor for receptacles, 48 inches for switches). Make sure the boxes protrude forward from the face of the studs so your drywall will be flush with the front of them. Once the boxes are in place, bore holes in the middle of the framing members.

YOU'LL NEED

TIME: 1 hour to install two boxes and run 10 feet of cable.

SKILLS: Drilling holes, fastening boxes in place.

TOOLS: Drill with spade bit, hammer, saw, lineman's pliers, chisel.

1 BORE THE HOLES TO RUN CABLE.

With an electric drill and a sharp ¾-inch spade bit, you can quickly bore holes for a run of cable. Keep extra bits on hand for large jobs. Align the holes by eye or use a chalk line to mark a guide. Bore as near the center of each stud as possible to maintain the strength of the framing and lessen the chance of drywall or trim nails piercing the cable.

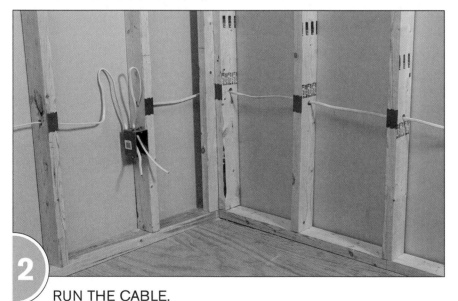

2 RUN THE CABLE.

Run the cable fairly taut so it does not hang between studs. At the corners you may need to bend the cable sharply to keep it at least 1¼ inches from the outer face of the framing.

Leave a loop of 6 to 8 inches of cable at each box. This loop provides a margin of error if the wire is damaged when stripped, and also makes future repairs and improvements easier.

3 ADD CABLE PROTECTORS.

If some of the holes end up less than 1¼ inches from the face of a framing member, attach a nail plate. Inexpensive and easy to install, it shields live electrical wires from being pierced by nails or screws. Tap the nail plate into place with a hammer.

4 CUT NOTCHES AT CORNERS.

If an inside corner is not solid wood, drill a hole in each direction. The two holes should intersect so you can thread the cable. Bend the cable and thread it through using a lineman's pliers to pull. If the corner is solid wood, use a handsaw or a reciprocating saw followed by a chisel to cut notches in either stud. Be sure to cover the notches with nailing plates.

5 TIGHTEN AND ATTACH THE CABLE.

Pull the cable fairly taut as you install it. At each box leave a 6- to 8-inch loop and attach the cable with an insulated staple.

6 DRILL PLATES FOR VERTICAL RUNS.

Drill holes in the top and bottom wall plates with a ¾-inch spade bit. Place the holes near the center of the plates. You may need to use a drill extension to bore through 2×4 plates. To avoid burning up the bit, stop periodically to let it cool. Drill at high speed and push gently.

7 RUN AND SECURE THE CABLE.

On vertical runs secure the cable with insulated staples about every 4 feet, wherever you change direction, and 8 to 12 inches from each box. Avoid sharp bends in the cable.

How you run cable in an attic depends on the attic's accessibility and usability. Some local codes allow cable to be surface-mounted in seldom-used spaces. Cable can be attached to the top of the joists with insulated staples. Then nail 1×2 guard strips on either side. These strips will protect the cable from damage if anyone steps on it or sets a heavy object on it.

RUNNING CABLE THROUGH HOLES.

If your attic is readily accessible, bore holes through the joists, at least 1½ inches below the top of the joists (see photo, near right). For the best protection—and to add a utilitarian floor—install plywood over joists. If the attic has flooring, remove some of it to install the cable, or take an alternate route along framing members. In a basement run cable through holes in the joists.

SPECIAL PROTECTION

Special rules may apply when running cable in permanently unfinished space. Check the local codes before you do any work. Some codes require protection for cable in an attic when it is within 6 feet of the entrance; in a garage or basement when it is within 8 feet of the floor. The most commonly accepted form of protection is conduit.

STRAPPING THICKER CABLE.

Because the heavy cable (8-gauge or larger) used for 240-volt appliance circuits is too stiff to thread easily through holes in joists, some codes allow wiring to be strapped to the underside of joists and along joist plates. Check your local code— conduit may be required for all exposed runs.

CONNECTING CABLE TO BOXES

Cable should be firmly connected to a box or to a nearby framing member. Consult local codes to find the method that your building department recommends. This page shows the most common methods for connecting nonmetallic cable to boxes. Other connectors are needed for armored cable, Greenfield, and conduit (see pages 151 and 154).

In most cases, it is easier to strip the sheathing--but not the wire insulation--before you run the cable into the box. Striping sheathing after the cable has been run into the box is tricky, and could cause the wire insulation to get nicked.

1 FEED CABLE INTO BOX.

Some plastic boxes have capture holes with spring fingers that grab the cable as you push it through. The capture hole keeps the cable from sliding back out of the box, but does not clamp the cable firmly.

½ inch of sheathing inside box

2 STAPLE CABLE TO FRAMING.

Secure the cable with an approved cable staple driven into the framing (usually, a stud). Codes usually require a staple within 8 inches of the box. Some codes require a cable loop between the staple and the box so you can pull more cable into the box in case of wire damage.

METAL BOX WITH SADDLE CLAMPS.

Some metal boxes come with internal saddle clamps. Tightening the saddle clamp's screw firmly secures one or two cables. Pull only one cable through each hole.

METAL BOX WITH CABLE CLAMPS.

Purchase cable clamps made for the type and size of cable you are running. Remove a knockout hole in the box. You can then attach the clamp to the box by tightening the locknut, run the cable through the clamp, and then tighten the two clamp screws to secure the cable. Or, you can first attach the clamp to the cable by tightening the two clamp screws, then run the cable into the box, and tighten the locknut.

METAL BOX WITH QUICK CLAMPS.

See that about ½ inch of sheathing is visible in the box; the clamp should grab the sheathing, not the wires. Twist the locknut on using your fingers, then push a straight screwdriver against the ears on the nut to tighten it.

PATCHING WALLS AND CEILINGS

When running cable through finished rooms, consult pages 140–143 and try to minimize damage to walls. Neatly cut holes in drywall, and keep the cutout pieces so you can replace them after the wiring is done. Plaster walls and ceilings are much more difficult to patch than drywall.

Before you start patching over your work, test the wiring thoroughly and have your building inspector review the work. If you cover the work before the inspection, you may be forced to tear out your patches.

A quality patching and painting job may take a full week. Usually at least three coats of joint compound must be applied, allowed to dry, and sanded smooth. Then the surface can be primed and painted to match the surrounding area.

YOU'LL NEED

TIME: About 1 hour to install each patch and apply the first coat; applying the second and third coats takes about 15 minutes each.

SKILLS: Basic carpentry skills, smoothing joint compound, painting.

TOOLS: Utility knife, hammer, drywall saw, drill, taping knives of several widths, corner taping blade, drywall sander with sandpaper or screens.

1 CUT BACKER PIECES TO FIT INTO THE HOLE.

Drywall patching kits make it easy to patch small holes, but for larger holes it's just as fast to install backerboards to support pieces of drywall. Cut the backer pieces from 1×4 lumber or strips of plywood about 6 inches longer than the width of the hole.

PATCHING MATERIALS

For strength use dry-mix joint compound for the first coat. (Do not use compound labeled "easy sand.") A bag labeled "90" will take about 90 minutes to harden; a bag labeled "45" will take 45 minutes to harden. You can apply additional coats of compound as soon as the first coat hardens, but you must wait longer for the compound to actually dry before you can paint. For additional coats apply ready-mix joint compound (it comes in a bucket), which is not strong but is easy to sand.

2 ATTACH THE BACKERS.

Slip each backer piece into the hole, center it, and hold it firm while you drive 1¼-inch screws into it through the surrounding drywall. If you saved the drywall pieces when you made the cutout, they will fit perfectly. Otherwise cut new drywall to fit.

3 PUT THE DRYWALL IN.

Scrape the patch edges free of loose paper and gypsum chunks. Attach the patches to the backers with screws. Sink the screwheads just below the surface of the paper face, but not deep enough to tear it. Cut pieces of fiberglass mesh tape to cover the joints; it's OK if an inch or so of a joint is not covered. Press the tape firmly onto the wall over the joints.

4 APPLY JOINT COMPOUND.

Mix a batch of joint compound so it is free of lumps and about the thickness of toothpaste. If your patch is at a corner, as shown, first use a drywall corner knife to apply compound. Concentrate on the inside corner; you will smooth the outer edges later.

5 FINISH TAPING.

Use a straight taping knife, at least 6 inches wide, to smooth the patch. Be patient; with practice you can become proficient. Feather the outer edges for a smooth transition to the wall. Allow the first coat to harden, then scrape away any protrusions.

6 APPLY ADDITIONAL COATS, THEN SAND.

Add a second coat, allow it to dry, then sand it smooth. To cut down on dust, you can use a damp sponge instead, although the result will be less smooth. Apply and sand succeeding coats until the surface feels smooth when you run your hand over it. Apply primer and paint.

1 TO REPAIR PLASTER, CUT OUT AND APPLY A DRYWALL PATCH.

Chip away all the loose plaster, including anything that feels spongy when you press on it, surrounding the hole. Measure the thickness of the plaster, and buy drywall that is no thicker. Take your time to cut a patch that fits the hole fairly neatly. Drive a series of 1¼-inch drywall screws through the drywall and into the lath.

2 TAPE THE JOINTS.

Fill the joints with joint compound, then apply mesh tape over the joints (see Step 3 on page 148). Apply a coat of joint compound over the tape, and follow the steps shown above to scrape the first coat and apply and smooth succeeding coats.

Flexible armored cable, or BX, is composed of a bendable metal sheathing containing insulated and ground wires. Greenfield, or flexible conduit, is a hollow flexible metal sheath. Like conduit, it is a tube that holds wires. Check local codes regarding the use of these materials since restrictions vary. (See page 125 for the different types of wire and cable available.)

1 NICK AND BEND THE CABLE.

Hold a hacksaw at a right angle to the spirals and just barely nick the sheathing. Be certain not to cut into the wire insulation inside. Bend the cable over and squeeze until it folds (see inset above).

2 COMPLETE THE CUT.

Twist the armor and it will snap free. The paper-wrapped wires (and aluminum bonding strip, if there is one) can be snipped with ordinary wire cutters. To expose the wires for connections to boxes and fixtures, cut off the armor at a second point about a foot away.

3 THREAD THROUGH HOLES IN FRAMING.

Run armored cable and flexible conduit through holes bored in the middle of framing members. Use notches where necessary. They are heavier and stiffer than nonmetallic cable, so it will take more room every time you want to change direction.

4 PROTECT THE CABLE.

Even armored sheathing can be pierced with a nail, so anywhere that the cable is within 1¼ inches of the framing surface, protect it with a nail plate. Check your local codes to see if short runs of flexible armored cable can be left exposed.

5 SECURE THE CABLE.

Support metal-clad cable with specially designed straps or staples approximately every 4 feet and within 12 inches of boxes. If you're fishing through existing walls or ceilings, secure the run as best you can.

CONNECTING ARMORED CABLE

1 CHOOSE THE CONNECTORS.

In most cases use a straight connector that holds the cable in place either by clamping it or with a setscrew. In some tight situations, you may need to use a 90-degree or 45-degree connector. To install a connector choose the side of the box you wish to access, and remove the knockout. Cut the cable to length and trim off the armored sheathing (see page 150).

2 INSTALL A BUSHING.

Pull the brown paper surrounding the wires back about an inch inside the armor. This leaves room to slip in a bushing. If your cable has a bonding strip, fold it back.

3 ATTACH THE CONNECTOR.

Slip on a connector, making sure the bushing is in place. Tighten the clamp or setscrew.

4 INSERT THE CONNECTOR.

Slip the wires and connector into a knockout hole, slip on a locknut, and tighten with your fingers. As with all wiring, connections should be made only in boxes.

5 TIGHTEN THE LOCKNUT.

Tighten the locknut with a hammer and screwdriver. Finally tug on the cable to make sure everything is securely fastened.

Codes sometimes require conduit, especially for exposed areas. Conduit has definite advantages: It protects the wires, and the electrical system can be upgraded later by pulling new wires through the conduit. Conduit is the most difficult way to install wiring because it's hard to bend. But it is still within reach for do-it-yourselfers. For small jobs use elbows and connectors at each turn to avoid bending conduit.

Codes allow many wires to be pulled through conduit. But the more wires you pull, the more crowded it gets, so buy larger conduit than required—say, ¾-inch instead of ½-inch.

YOU'LL NEED

TIME: About 2 hours for a run with three bends and two boxes.

SKILLS: Careful measuring, clean cutting, screwing pieces together.

TOOLS: Hacksaw, pliers, screwdriver, conduit reamer.

1 MEASURE AND CUT.
Measure the distance for the run—don't forget to subtract for the connector or elbow you will be using. Cut conduit with a hacksaw or a tubing cutter. Hold conduit against a cleat, or use a miter box to keep it from rolling as you saw.

2 REAM THE ENDS.
Cutting with a tubing cutter or hacksaw leaves burrs inside the end of the conduit that can chew up wiring insulation in a hurry. Remove them from the inside of the conduit using a conduit reamer. Smooth rough spots on the outside as well so the conduit can slip easily into a connector.

3 INSTALL A JUNCTION BOX.
Where you have more than four turns to negotiate, install a junction box. When it's time to pull the wires, it will let you start another run. More boxes and few bends ease wire-pulling.

ADD AN OFFSET.
Use an offset connector to keep the conduit flush against the wall when it's attached to a box. The conduit can be bent to form an offset (see page 153), but adding an offset connector is easier.

4 INSTALL PULLING ELBOWS.
A pulling elbow makes negotiating corners easier. Remove the cover to pull the wires through. Don't make any connections inside a pulling elbow; wires must pass through without a break.

BENDING CONDUIT

For larger jobs it is expensive and time-consuming to use connectors at each corner. Instead bend the conduit. Bending isn't difficult although getting the bend in just the right location is tricky and requires some practice.

Runs begin and end at places where you can get at wires to pull them. Codes generally forbid a total of more than 360 degrees of bends in a run. Before you start bending add up the degrees of the bends you'll be making in a single run to ensure the total is less than 360 degrees.

YOU'LL NEED

TIME: About 30 minutes to measure, bend a piece, and connect it on either end.

SKILLS: This is a specialized skill that requires practice.

TOOLS: Conduit bender, tape measure, black marking pen.

1 MEASURE FOR A CORNER.

To get conduit around a corner, first measure from the box to the top of the bend (distance A). Then subtract the bend distance and mark the conduit. (The bend distance for ½-inch conduit is 5 inches. For ¾- and 1-inch conduit, allow 6 and 8 inches, respectively.) Slip the conduit bender onto the tubing and align it as shown.

2 MAKE THE BEND.

With one foot on the rear of the bender, pull slowly and steadily on the handle. Be careful. Tugging too sharply will crimp the tubing and you'll have to start over with another piece. (Codes forbid installing crimped conduit.) Making crimp-free bends takes practice, so don't be surprised if your first efforts fail. After making the bend trim section B by holding the bent conduit in place for measuring. Cut the end so it reaches the box.

START AN OFFSET WITH A 15-DEGREE BEND...

When mounting conduit on a flat surface, you'll need to form an offset at each box. Offsets must be aligned with other bends in the tubing. A stripe painted along the length of the conduit helps you do this. First make a 15-degree bend.

THEN BEND IN THE OTHER DIRECTION.

Roll the conduit over and move the bender a few inches farther from the end. Then pull until the section beyond the first bend is parallel to the floor.

USE COUPLINGS TO JOIN SECTIONS.

To join sections end to end, use either securely fitted setscrew or compression couplings.

> ## ⚠ CAUTION
>
> Make all connections mechanically strong. Pulling wires through conduit can put a strain on connections. Grounding depends on secure metal-to-metal connections.

ANCHOR THE CONDUIT.

Anchor conduit runs with at least one strap every 8 feet and a strap within 3 feet of every box. For masonry walls use screws and plastic anchors. When attaching to framing, drive barbed straps into the wood.

To mount conduit inside walls, bore holes in the studs, or notch the framing and secure it with straps or metal plates every 8 feet.

CONNECT TO BOXES.

Box connectors differ mainly in the way they attach to conduit. Compression connectors grab the conduit as you tighten the nut with a wrench. To install a setscrew connector, slip it on and tighten the screw.

All these connectors attach to the box with the same threaded stud and locknut arrangement used with cable connectors (see page 147). Insert the stud into a knockout hole, turn the locknut finger tight, then tap the nut with a hammer and screwdriver to tighten it. A two-piece connector comes in handy when space is tight inside a box. Instead of a locknut it has a compression fitting. As you tighten the nut, the fitting squeezes the conduit.

Compression connector

Two-piece connector

Setscrew connector

Angled compression connector

Now comes the moment when you realize why codes are so specific about bends, crimps, and burrs in conduit. Pulling wire can be surprisingly hard work. If you suspect that the wire is scraping against something that might damage the insulation, stop work, locate the trouble spot (you can find it easily by using the wire as a measuring device), and remove it. Purchase pulling grease to lubricate the wires if you need to make a long pull.

YOU'LL NEED

TIME: A few minutes to an hour to pull wires through a conduit run.

SKILLS: Basic electrical skills.

TOOLS: Screwdriver, lineman's pliers, fish tape.

1 PUSH THROUGH SHORT RUNS.

For short runs with only a couple of bends, you can probably push the wires from one box to the other. Feed the wires carefully to protect the insulation.

2 ATTACH A FISH TAPE.

If you can't push the wires, you'll need a fish tape and an assistant. Snake the fish tape through the conduit, hook the wires to the fish tape and secure with electrician's tape. Wrap the connection neatly so it can slide through the conduit.

3 PULL THE WIRES THROUGH.

As one worker feeds the wire in and makes sure there are no kinks, the other pulls. Pull the wires with steady pressure—avoid tugging. As the wires work past bends, expect to employ more muscle. If you have lots of wires or a long pull, lubricate the wires with pulling grease. Where possible use gravity to aid the process. Feed the wires from above and pull from below.

4 LEAVE PLENTY OF WIRE IN THE BOX.

Leave 6 to 8 inches of wire at each box. Never splice wire inside conduit—all wires must run continuously from box to box.

GLOSSARY

For more information refer to the index on pages 158–160.

Amp (A). A measurement of the amount of electrical current in a circuit at any moment. See Volt and Watt.

Armored cable. Two or more insulated wires wrapped in a protective metal sheathing.

Ballast. Transformer that steps up the voltage in a fluorescent lamp.

Bell wire. A thin wire used for doorbells. Typically 18-gauge.

Bimetal. Two metals that expand and contract at different rates to open or close a circuit automatically. They are commonly used in circuit breakers and thermostats.

Box. A metal or plastic enclosure within which connections are made and on which devices are mounted.

Bus bar. A main power terminal to which circuits are attached in a fuse or breaker box. One bus bar serves the circuit's hot side, the other the neutral side.

BX. An older type of armored cable that contains no ground wire. In a typical installation the metal sheathing itself acts as the ground.

Cable. Two or more insulated conductors wrapped in metal or plastic outer sheathing.

Circuit. The path of electrical flow from a power source through an outlet and back to ground.

Circuit breaker. A switch that automatically interrupts electrical flow in a circuit in case of an overload or short circuit.

Codes. Local laws governing safe wiring practices. See National Electrical Code.

Common. A terminal on a three-way switch, usually with a dark-colored screw and marked COM.

Conductor. A wire or anything else that carries electricity.

Conduit. Rigid or flexible tubing through which wires are run.

Contact. The point where two electrical conductors touch.

Continuity tester. A device that tells whether a circuit is complete and capable of carrying electricity.

Delayed-start tube. A type of fluorescent tube that takes a few seconds to warm up.

Derate. To lower total service capacity because not all the appliances and fixtures on a circuit are used at the same time.

Device. A switch or receptacle.

Dimmer. A switch that lets you vary the intensity of a light.

Duplex receptacle. A device that includes two plug outlets. Most receptacles in homes are duplexes.

Electrical metallic tubing (EMT). Thin-walled, rigid conduit suitable for indoor use.

Electrons. Invisible particles of charged matter moving at the speed of light through an electrical conductor.

End-wired. A wiring configuration, also called end-line wiring or switch-loop wiring, in which power runs first to the fixture box, and a loop of wire runs to the switch box. See through-switch wiring.

Fishing. Getting cables through finished walls and ceilings.

Fish tape. A long strip of spring steel used for fishing cables and for pulling wires through conduit.

Fixture. Any light or other electrical device permanently attached to a home's wiring.

Flexible metal conduit. Tubing that can be bent easily by hand. See Greenfield.

Fluorescent tube. A light source that uses an ionization process to produce ultraviolet radiation. This becomes visible light when it hits the coated inner surface of the tube.

Four-way switch. A type of switch used to control a light from three or more locations.

Fuse. A safety device designed to stop electrical flow if a circuit shorts or is overloaded. Like a circuit breaker, a fuse protects against fire from overheated wiring.

Ganging. Assembling two or more electrical components into a single unit. Boxes, switches, and receptacles often are ganged.

General-purpose circuit. Serves several light and/or receptacle outlets. See Heavy-duty circuit and Small-appliance circuit.

Greenfield. Flexible metal conduit through which wires are pulled.

Ground. Refers to the fact that electricity always seeks the shortest possible path to the earth. Neutral wires carry electricity to ground in all circuits. An additional grounding wire, or the sheathing of metal-clad cable or conduit, protects against shock from a malfunctioning device.

Ground fault circuit interrupter (GFCI). A safety device that senses any shock hazard and shuts down a circuit or receptacle.

Heavy-duty circuit. Serves just one 120- to 240-volt appliance. See General-purpose circuit and Small-appliance circuit.

Hot wire. The conductor that carries current to a receptacle or other outlet. See Ground and Neutral wire.

Incandescent bulb. Light source with a metal filament that glows at white heat.

Insulation. A nonconductive covering that protects wires and other electricity carriers.

Junction box. An enclosure used for splitting circuits into different branches. In a junction box wires connect only to each other, never to a switch, receptacle, or fixture.

Kilowatt (kw). One thousand watts. A kilowatt hour is the standard measure of electrical consumption.

Knockouts. Tabs that can be removed to make openings in a box. The openings accommodate cable and conduit connectors.

LB connector or fitting. Elbow for conduit with access for pulling wires.

Leads. Short wires.

MC cable. Armored cable that contains a ground wire, usually green-insulated.

National Electrical Code (NEC). A set of rules governing safe wiring methods drafted by the National Fire Protection Association. Local codes sometimes differ from and take precedence over the NEC.

Neon tester. A device with two leads and a small bulb that determines whether a circuit is carrying current.

Neutral wire. A conductor that carries current from an outlet back to ground. It is clad in white insulation. See Ground and Hot wire.

Nonmetallic sheathed cable. Two or more insulated conductors clad in a plastic covering.

Outlet. Any potential point of use in a circuit, including receptacles, switches, and light fixtures.

Overload. The condition when a circuit carries more amperage than it was designed to handle. Overloading causes wires to heat up and blows fuses or trips circuit breakers.

Polarized plugs. Plugs designed so the hot and neutral sides of a circuit can't be accidentally reversed. One prong of the plug is wider or a different shape than the other.

Raceway wiring. Surface-mounted channels for extending circuits.

Rapid-start tubes. Fluorescent tubes that light up almost instantly.

Receptacle. An outlet that supplies power for lamps and other plug-in devices.

Rigid conduit. Metal tubing to contain wires. It can be bent only with a special tool.

Romex. A trade name for nonmetallic-sheathed cable.

Service entrance. The point where power enters a home.

Service panel. The main fuse or breaker box in a home.

Short circuit. A condition that occurs when hot and neutral wires contact each other. Fuses and breakers protect against fire, which can result from a short.

Small-appliance circuit. Usually has only two or three 20-amp receptacle outlets.

Solderless connectors. Screw-on or crimp-type devices to join two wires.

Stripping. Removing insulation from wire or sheathing from cable.

Stud. An electrical connector. (Also a term referring to a framing member.)

Subpanel. A smaller, subsidiary fuse or breaker box.

System ground. A wire connecting a service panel to the earth. It may be attached to a main water pipe or to a rod driven into the ground.

Three-way switch. Operates a light from two locations.

Time-delay fuse. A fuse that does not break the circuit during a momentary overload. If the overload continues the fuse blows.

Through-wired. A wiring configuration in which power travels first through the switch box and then on to the fixture. See End-wired.

Transformer. A device that reduces or increases voltage. In home wiring, transformers step down current for use with low-voltage equipment such as thermostats and doorbell systems.

Travelers. The conductors that run between three-way switches.

Underwriters knot. A knot used to secure wires in a lamp socket.

Underwriters Laboratories (UL). Independent testing agency that examines electrical components for safety hazards.

Volt (V). A measure of electrical pressure. Volts × amps = watts.

Voltmeter. A device that measures voltage in a circuit.

Wall box. A rectangular enclosure for receptacles and switches. See Junction box.

Watt (W). A measure of the power an electrical device consumes; volts × amps. See Amp, Kilowatt, and Volt.

INDEX

Index *(continued)*

METRIC CONVERSIONS

U.S. Units to Metric Equivalents

To convert from	Multiply by	To Get
Inches	25.4	Millimeters
Inches	2.54	Centimeters
Feet	30.48	Centimeters
Feet	.03048	Meters
Yards	.9144	Meters
Miles	1.6093	Kilometers
Square inches	6.4516	Square centimeters
Square feet	0.0929	Square meters
Square yards	0.8361	Square meters
Acres	0.4047	Hectares
Square miles	2.5899	Square kilometers
Cubic inches	16.387	Cubic centimeters
Cubic feet	0.0283	Cubic meters
Cubic feet	28.316	Liters
Cubic yards	0.7646	Cubic meters
Cubic yards	764.55	Liters

Metric Units to U.S. Equivalents

To convert from	Multiply by	To Get
Millimeters	0.0394	Inches
Centimeters	0.3937	Inches
Centimeters	0.0328	Feet
Meters	3.2808	Feet
Meters	1.0936	Yards
Kilometers	0.6214	Miles
Square centimeters	0.1550	Square inches
Square meters	10.764	Square feet
Square meters	1.1960	Square yards
Hectares	2.4711	Acres
Square kilometers	0.3861	Square miles
Cubic centimeters	0.0610	Cubic inches
Cubic meters	35.315	Cubic feet
Liters	0.0353	Cubic feet
Cubic meters	1.038U	Cubic yards
Liters	0.0013	Cubic yards

To convert from degrees Fahrenheit (F) to degrees Celsius (C), first subtract 32, then multiply by ⅝.

To convert from degrees Celsius to degrees Fahrenheit, multiply by ⅝, then add 32.